HER
MAJESTY'S
WILL

This is a work of fiction. All of the characters, events, and organizations portrayed in this work are either products of the authors' imagination or used fictitiously.

Her Majesty's Will

Copyright © 2017 by Robert Kauzlaric

Based on the novel by David Blixt, published in 2012 by Sordelet Ink.

Cover by Robert Kauzlaric and David Blixt

ISBN-13: 978-1944540289
ISBN-10: 1-944540288

For information about production rights, e-mail:
rob@lifelinetheatre.com

Published by Sordelet Ink

HER MAJESTY'S WILL

ADAPTED FOR THE STAGE BY
ROBERT KAUZLARIC

FROM THE NOVEL BY
DAVID BLIXT

Published by
Sordelet Ink

Her Majesty's Will received its world premiere at Lifeline Theatre in Chicago, IL, on June 6, 2017. It was directed by Chris Hainsworth; costume design was by Aly Renee Amidei; fight direction was by David Blixt; lighting design was by Diane D. Fairchild; scenic design was by Eleanor Kahn; properties design was by Alec Long; original music and sound design was by Jeffrey Levin; assistant directors were Sarah Scanlon and Caitlin McManus; and the production stage manager was Kate Reed. The cast was as follows:

Javier Ferreira - Will
Bryan Bosque - Kit
Heather Chrisler - Chorus, Huffing Kate, Helena of Snakenborg, Em
LaQuin Groves - Savage, Audience Member 2, Driver,
Ruffler, Lucy Soldier 1
Martel Manning - Phelippes, Audience Member 3, Innkeeper, Lyly,
Dibdale, Evans, Actor Playing The Noble-Man
Dan Cobbler - Actor Playing Revenge, Tarlton, Cripplegate Guard 2,
"Poor Tom", Lucy, Actor Playing Horatio
Peter Greenberg - Actor Playing Hieronymo, Blacke Davie,
Cripplegate Guard 3, Greene, Stagehand
Don Bender - Boy, Higgins, Actor Playing The Ghost of Andrea,
Walsingham, Gifford, Lucy Solider 2, Augustine
Mike Ooi - Rookwood, Audience Member 1, Cripplegate Guard 1,
Cutting Ball, Actor Playing Bel-Imperia

Understudies
Justin Harner, Maggie Patchett, Cole Simon, Sean Sinitski, & Tony St. Clair

The following credit must appear in all programs/playbills handed to audience members at performances of *Her Majesty's Will*:

HER MAJESTY'S WILL WAS ORIGINALLY PRODUCED BY
LIFELINE THEATRE, CHICAGO, ILLINOIS, IN 2017.

lifeline

THEATRE
Big Stories, Up Close

Cast of Characters

PLAYWRIGHTS

WILLIAM SHAKESPEARE: *A young man, passionate and bold; later, the greatest playwright that ever lived.*

CHRISTOPHER "KIT" MARLOWE: *A charming, self-obsessed rogue; later, another legendary playwright.*

JOHN LYLY: *One of the Wits; a lean and proper playwright, poet, and proponent of Euphuism.*

ROBERT GREENE: *One of the Wits; a grossly fat playwright, scholar and drunkard.*

LONDON ROGUES & RASCALS

DICK TARLTON: *The Queen's favorite fool, stocky, with a cheerfully ruddy face.*

CUTTING BALL: *A shifty thief with the jaw of a mastiff and the eyes of a hawk.*

EM BALL: *Cutting Ball's crafty sister.*

HUFFING KATE: *A perpetually angry wench who speaks in loud, angry gusts.*

BLACKE DAVIE: *A massive man with a bristling black beard and wild eyes.*

AN INNKEEPER: *At the Elephant & Castle.*

"POOR TOM": *A madman from Bethlam Royal Hospital.*

A RUFFLER: *Outside Gifford's house.*

NOBLES & THEIR GUARDS

HELENA OF SNAKENBORG: *Marchioness of Northampton and Lady-in-Waiting to Queen Elizabeth.*

SIR THOMAS LUCY: *A knight and Catholic-hunter; a pasty fellow with curly hair like a topiary.*

CRIPPLEGATE GUARDS 1, 2 & 3: *Soldiers at Cripplegate.*

TWO SOLDIERS: *In service to Lucy.*

DRIVER: *Of Lady Helena's carriage.*

IN HER MAJESTY'S SECRET SERVICE

SIR FRANCIS WALSINGHAM: *The Queen's master of spies; black of hair, black of beard, and black of eye.*

THOMAS PHELIPPES: *A spy and forger in the service of Walsingham.*

SOLDIER: *At Seething Lane.*

CATHOLIC REBELS

JOHN SAVAGE: *A violent Catholic thug with a carbuncle nose.*

GILBERT GIFFORD: *A disgraced deacon.*

ROBERT DIBDALE: *A Catholic priest, originally from Warwickshire.*

MATTHEW ROOKWOOD: *A Catholic agent; branded with the murderer's M on his cheek.*

FRANCIS HIGGINS: *A Catholic agent; wears an eyepatch.*

LANCASHIRE LOCALS
  BOY: *The offstage voice of a boy in Will's school.*

THEATRE-FOLK
  HENRY EVANS: *The prompter at the Newington Butts Theatre; a wiry, fussy man.*
  AUGUSTINE: *An experienced actor at the Newington Butts.*
  STAGEHAND: *At the Newington Butts; a former sailor.*
  AUDIENCE MEMBERS 1, 2 & 3: *At the Newington Butts.*
  ACTOR PLAYING THE GHOST OF ANDREA
  ACTOR PLAYING REVENGE
  ACTOR PLAYING HIERONYMO
  ACTOR PLAYING BEL-IMPERIA
  ACTOR PLAYING HORATIO
  ACTOR PLAYING THE NOBLE-MAN

THEATRICAL DEVICES
  CHORUS: *Prologue, Chorus, Time, and Epilogue in one.*

Other roles, as needed (Soldiers, Guards, Laborers, Layabouts, Londoners) are
played by the ensemble.

SETTING

Multiple locations in and around Lancashire and London
July & August, 1586.

ACT I
ART'S FALSE BORROWED FACE

(The CHORUS enters)

CHORUS

Join us now – for a tale of lords and ladies, poets and paupers, wenches and wits... with a mighty monarch looming o'er the swelling scene. But who are we to tell this tale? Can we, with our simple craft, cram within these confines the peaty bogs and rolling drumlins of Lancashire? Can we conjure the alleys and ale-houses of an erstwhile London? O! Let our devices burn like stars across the midnight of your imaginations. Fill our taverns with rowdy roughspuns. Press into our streets the rude, ragged rabble. And see, in us – merely shadows – the legends of yesteryear. We begin far north of London, that center of the known world. Enter: the greatest theatrical visionary the world has ever known... *(Grandly)* William Shakespeare!

(Lights rise on WILL. Over a schoolmaster's gown he is costumed as a woman: lumpy false bosoms beneath an ill-fitting dress, an unkempt wig clinging to his head. It is not a dignified moment)

CHORUS
In the long history of inauspicious beginnings, few can rival that of young Will, grappling with the Greeks in a one-room schoolhouse.

WILL
(As Calonike, in a woman's voice) O! Lysistrata, it's so hard for women—

BOY
(Offstage) It's getting hard, all right!

(The sound of many laughing boys is heard. WILL pulls off his wig and switches to his own voice)

WILL
Now, boys... Boys! Quiet down! I realize none of you want to play girls, but if you don't get up here and do this play for me today, you'll do it tomorrow... for your fathers.

(A chorus of groans and objections is heard from the boys. WILL removes the dress)

CHORUS
Some are born great. Some seize greatness. And some discover the greatness within only by passing through the crucibles of Time and Incident. So, forget what you know – what you think you know – of the "Bard of Avon." It is July, 1586, and there is no "Bard." No legend. No legacy. There is only... a man unformed. A man afraid. A man who daren't dream of the future while he's yet hiding from his past. And admit me, Chorus,

to this history – not of William Shakespeare, but of Will Falstaff – and gently hear, kindly judge, our play. *(She exits)*

WILL

Boys, I know it may seem silly; but the words – the ideas – are not. Theatre is the gateway to understanding humanity. It's not about story; stories can be told in a thousand ways: song, prose, even dance. Theatre is about character. It's the act of bringing people to life. Keeping them alive. This play was written two thousand years ago. The people in it are long dead and buried. But each time it's performed, they breathe again. As an actor, you are... a god, breathing life into a statue!

(A woman's scream is heard from outside, followed by the sound of men cursing and struggling)

WILL

What was that? Slip out the back way, lads. Hurry, now.

(WILL grabs a sword from behind his desk and goes outside. On the late afternoon road, two rough men – SAVAGE and ROOKWOOD – are struggling with a DARK LADY dressed all in black)

SAVAGE

(To ROOKWOOD) Find it!

ROOKWOOD

(Aggressively searching the DARK LADY) Where be it, whore?

WILL

Release the lady, you varlets!

(ROOKWOOD grabs the DARK LADY and covers her mouth. SAVAGE steps forth, hand on his rapier's hilt)

SAVAGE
Sod off.

WILL
(Bringing his blade up into the basic invitation)
Release her, I say, and be gone.

ROOKWOOD
What does a schoolmaster know of fighting?

WILL
I wear a schoolmaster's gown today, but that is the fault of this blade. I swore never again to raise it in anger, but if you fail to release the lady I will sing this sword through a measure of crimson music until my forte is cadent with your intermingled sanguinity.

ROOKWOOD
(After a blank stare) Huh?

WILL
Let her go or I'll kill you. I was trying to be—

SAVAGE
Leave off. We're on orders to bring this thieving wench back to our mistress.

WILL
Your mistress is no lady, to send such as you to retrieve her in this manner.

SAVAGE
She's a traitor, with stolen property on her person.

WILL
That's for the law to consider. And if you persist, it must perforce consider your deaths at my hand.

(For a tense moment, SAVAGE studies WILL. Then the DARK LADY bites ROOKWOOD's hand and slips out of his clutches. SAVAGE steps forward, but WILL passes into the second invitation)

WILL
Step inside, my lady.

DARK LADY
A hero, true! *(She kisses WILL fiercely and exits into the schoolhouse)*

SAVAGE
We'll be back. With a writ.

WILL
Begone!

ROOKWOOD
And she'd better be here when—

(WILL makes a threatening move, cutting off ROOKWOOD's bluster. SAVAGE and ROOKWOOD slink away. When they're out of sight, WILL's posture of bravery collapses)

WILL
What have I done?

(WILL re-enters the house and goes to his loft, discovering a half-dressed KIT putting on WILL's clothes)

WILL
Who are you, sirrah, and what have you done with the maiden?

KIT
I murdered her. And she was no maiden, I assure
you.

WILL
*(Discovering a discarded wig, bum roll, false bosom,
and dress beside the bed)* Pray tell me you are not
she.

KIT
I am not, though I was. But since she is no more,
I needs must be myself. *(Pulling a shirt over his
head)* A thousand thanks. If they'd continued in
their hunt they'd have found more than they
sought.

WILL
Wait – are those mine? Did you just steal my
clothes?

KIT
Your generous donation is greatly appreciated.
May I know the name of my benefactor?

WILL
William Sh... *(Almost forgetting to lie)* Will
Falstaff.

KIT
A delight. *(With a bow)* I was Kitty, but now it's
back to Kit. Kat for Kit, Tat for Tit. *(Examining
his shirt)* Eww. Give me that shirt. This one will
never do.

WILL
Why not?

KIT
It's soiled! *(With a batting of eyelashes)* Will you

not offer your finest to a damsel in distress?

(They swap shirts. During the exchange, KIT notices that WILL's back is covered with angry red scars)

KIT
Someone's been naughty, I see...

(WILL hastily dons the other shirt without responding)

KIT
(Fussing with his outfit, making himself presentable)
Much better. Have you a pistol?

WILL
No.

KIT
Alas! But a man with such skill at fence must disdain the hackbut as a vile tool.

WILL
I am no swordsman, I must confess.

KIT
No? But you handled yourself with such excellent poise, my brave champion. Why, you performed the imbrokata so well I was tempted to applaud!

WILL
The imbrokata?

KIT
The last invitation you issued: knuckles up, wrist high, point down.

WILL
I just saw it done once and practiced until I thought I had it right.

KIT
I assumed you were a swordsman, and instead you are an actor! Bravo!

WILL
I'm no–

KIT
O! Don't be modest. How delightful to find a kindred soul here in the blasted North. If that's where I am. Where am I?

WILL
Lancashire. You don't know where you are?

KIT
I am in Lancashire. And I spy in you, William my Conqueror, a kinship. There are certain men who seem to be that which they are not. I can recreate much that I observe with very little effort, and with significantly more style. Is it the same for you?

WILL
(Uncertain how much he should confide) Perhaps...

KIT
What can you do?

WILL
Well... juggling, tumbling, voices–

KIT
Marvelous. You'll be so useful! Now, hurry and pack. (Gathering the remains of his disguise in a bundle) We must be gone before the foe returns in greater numbers.

WILL
I can't leave. I'm hired to run this school the

whole year.

KIT
You must leave. My pursuers are in deadly
earnest.

WILL
Then we'll go to the authorities.

KIT
We'll do no such thing! I'd have to impart the
intelligence I've gathered. And once they hear
of treason—

WILL
Treason?!

KIT
Aye, you're embroiled in a dangerous game of
treason now. And when a nobleman hears what
I would speak, a vision will descend upon him,
like the angels to the prophets. He'll not see us
in the part of the hero, but himself, and we'll be
hanged.

WILL
Why would they hang me?

KIT
The moment you drew on my assailants you
became my accomplice.

WILL
What have you gotten me involved in?

KIT
(*Producing a wax seal with a flattened face*) Behold
the private seal of Lord Walsingham, spymaster
and chief counselor to Her Majesty Elizabeth.

KIT & WILL
(*A personal expression of genuine loyalty*) Long may
she reign.

KIT
The dangers are real, but we're off to save a
nation, and perhaps her queen. You wouldn't say
'no' to the Queen, would you?

WILL
No. Never. Of course not.

KIT
She needs you.

WILL
Then I'm your man.

KIT
Also, we can expect to be rewarded beyond our
wildest dreams. (*Spanking WILL playfully*) And
my dreams are wickedly wild.

(*The sound of distant horses is heard from the road*)

KIT
We must fly!

(*Not quite knowing what's happening to him, WILL
throws some belongings into a satchel*)

WILL
Where are we going?

KIT
If you're taken, it's best you know nothing of
our destination. Come! We'll travel by night and
hide by day.

(*They walk overnight and pass the better part of the*

next day sleeping in an overgrown wood. As the sun sinks low on the horizon and a chill fog rolls in, KIT and WILL break down their camp)

KIT
Lord, but the North is a dismal kind of place, is it not?

WILL
Lancashire's not really "the North"...

KIT
I have no idea where I am, honestly. Two days ago I was a serving wench in Staffard—

WILL
(With a sudden flush of panic) Stratford?

KIT
No, no, Staffordshire. *(Studying WILL for a moment)* Stratford. Is that your home?

WILL
My birthplace.

KIT
And...? *(When WILL doesn't reply)* And you're also on the run, I see. Intriguing. Tell me more. Tell me. Tell me.

(WILL breaks away)

KIT
No? Very well. So, I was in Staffordshire – miles from Stratford – pretending to be the creature you met me as.

WILL
Why were you in such a guise?

KIT
To gain intelligence against the insidious foe.
The castle was rife with treason. When I obtained
evidence to prove said treason, I fled.

WILL
If they catch us... could we really be gallowed?

KIT
They're on the hunt for a man and a woman.
Who will notice two fine fellows out for an
evening stroll? All will be well. Come. *(He tosses
the rapier to WILL)* Take this up. If you're going
to be of any use in a real fight, it's time for your
first true lesson in swordsmanship. *(Taking up a
stick)* Ah-ha! The very thing.

*(KIT adopts a stance with the stick held loosely in
his grip. WILL takes a pose he used the day before)*

KIT
Good, though a trifle more bend in the knees.
Excellent. Now, when you think of fighting,
what do you see in your mind's eye?

WILL
Blood. And... well, mostly blood.

KIT
Yes, there may be blood, if the thing's done right.
But picture, rather, a dance.

WILL
A dance?

KIT
Absolutely. *(Demonstrating)* Fighting is danc-
ing. There is a sequence of accepted steps. And
there is always a leader. That's the role you must

assume if you can.

WILL
Where did you learn all this?

KIT
At college. Now, come! *(He leads WILL through a series of killing and wounding strokes)* Very good – you're a natural! Around, around! The punto is a circular step, not an advance. And the blade follows the same arc, around com ca, and za! The point is buried just below your opponent's shapely buttock. *(He spanks WILL with his stick)*

WILL
Enough! *(He whips around, knocks KIT to the ground, and puts him on point)*

KIT
Hey! I was teaching you!

WILL
It's time I learned more about our cause, Kit. Well, let's begin with that. What's your Christian name?

KIT
Christopher – a name I never enjoyed. So often I heard it in tones of need or disapproval. *(Demonstrating)* Christopher. Christopher! *(He suddenly beats away WILL's blade and springs to his feet, jabbing playfully at WILL)* In Kit I discovered a wondrous freedom: freedom from inflection. Kit. Kit. You see? It's quite past the hedge of the teeth before it can be laden with want. It's impossible to imbue Kit with overtones or undercurrents. *(A series of blows ends them frozen coeur a coeur)* You are equally fortunate in Will,

though my... *(Pressing against WILL)* hard, deci-
sive ending is better than your almost indefinite
one.

WILL
Don't try to distract me. How did you come into
this sordid business?

KIT
You wish to hear The Most Lamentable Historie
of Christopher Marlowe? Very well. Attend. *(He
"takes the stage" to tell his story)* As a schoolmaster, you'll appreciate the irony–

WILL
Former schoolmaster. May I never set foot in a
schoolroom again.

KIT
Well, my troubles likewise stem from education.
My father sent me to Cambridge, where – and
I'm certain you'll find this difficult to credit – I
was something of a rakehell.

WILL
(In mock surprise) No!

KIT
'Tis true. I was nothing like the sober, respect-
able fellow you've come to adore so quickly. I
committed an indiscretion – whoops! – and was
on the brink of expulsion when I was snatched
back from the precipice by... not a savior, but...
*(KIT pulls his black skirt from the pack and fashions
a dark hood from it)* A fiend. A man of great power.
It seems that Cambridge is a breeding ground
for government agents.

WILL
You were offered your degree, in exchange for
a service.

KIT
Hardly. I was banished to France. And forced to
act as a spy. The assumption was that a man of my
talents could infiltrate societies closed to their
usual agents.

WILL
I see.

KIT
Paris proved far from unpleasant, and I enjoyed
much amusement. However, after a year abroad,
I learned that in Staffordshire there was a chance
to deliver to my government masters such a coup
as would put them forever in my debt. It meant
returning to England – against orders – and
taking on a guise no mortal actor could endure.

WILL
How long did you pretend to be a woman?

KIT
(With pride) A fortnight.

WILL
And you weren't discovered?

KIT
Not even suspected! I am a god among actors.
I've maintained one guise or another for all my
life! *(A shadow of melancholy briefly falls over him)*
I sometimes fear that beneath it all there's no
real me, just another player waiting for his roll.
All the world's a stage, Will. Our parts depend

upon our setting, and the expectations of our audience. You enjoy theatre?

KIT

WILL
I love plays, yes. But I've never been in an actual theatre.

KIT
But you have clearly performed!

WILL
In school, a little. And once, as a child, I said some lines when a traveling troupe came through town. But get back to your story. You returned from Paris to foil some plot. What plot? And did your masters know?

KIT
You mean my backbiting tormentors? No. I preferred to present them with a fait accompli. So I used my disguise to infiltrate the castle and showed the men there what they expected to see: a wench of no standing, willing to perform any act to gain advancement.

WILL
You can't mean—

KIT
Ah, Will! Let us agree that sex is a woman's best weapon, and I would have been a fool not to make use of it.

WILL
But surely they discovered that you lacked... or, rather, had...

KIT
Have you never taken the pleasure of a hurried

pinch in a forgotten corner, the fear of discovery adding spice to the act? Clothes are rarely removed, and when pushing and pulling there are means of managing. Besides, there are other ways... But I'm embarrassing you.

WILL
It's getting dark, we should get on the road–

KIT
Come, do not deny that you and I shared a spark upon our meeting. Shall I resume my wig and bosoms? Is that the way to tempt you?

WILL
I thought you a woman.

KIT
What is woman but the woe of man? *(Taking WILL's hand)* Remove the woman, remove the woe.

WILL
Kit, I...

KIT
(Abruptly pulling WILL to the ground and covering his mouth) They've found us!

(SAVAGE enters, leading ROOKWOOD and HIGGINS. All are armed)

SAVAGE
Any sign of them?

ROOKWOOD
(Discovering Will and Kit's bags) Someone was here. They must be close.

(WILL tries to stealthily move towards his sword, but

is spotted by SAVAGE)

SAVAGE
If it isn't our fierce schoolmaster! We're ready to learn you a lesson or two. *(Putting WILL on point)* Where's the woman? Tell me true, and I might let you live.

WILL
(To SAVAGE) Look, I... I... *(He catches sight of a crucifix hanging from a cord around SAVAGE's neck. He smacks SAVAGE's sword aside and grabs the crucifix)* Idiot! How dare you wear this crucifix openly? Do you wish to bring death upon us all?

SAVAGE
Don't you take on airs with me—

WILL
How could I not, when you befoul the air with your every utterance!

SAVAGE
I don't know who you think you are—

WILL
I'll make known to you what I am, and all will become clear. *(He raises his right hand and makes an elaborate series of three gestures)* In nomine Patris, et Filii, et Spiritus Sancti.

(Everyone gasps. SAVAGE and his companions lower their weapons and repeat the sign WILL gave)

SAVAGE, ROOKWOOD & HIGGINS
In nomine Patris, et Filii, et Spiritus Sancti.

(As the CATHOLIC AGENTS approach to gather around the campsite, KIT briefly pulls WILL aside)

KIT
(Aside to WILL) Is that some secret Catholic
sign? How did you—

WILL
(Aside to KIT) Later!

SAVAGE
Forgive us, brother. We didn't know.

WILL
How could you? My posting was God's doing. I
believe introductions are in order.

SAVAGE
I'm John Savage. That's Rookwood. Higgins, go
watch the road.

(HIGGINS takes up a sentry position)

WILL
My name is...

*(As WILL searches for a name, KIT swoops in.
Bowing with a flourish, he speaks in a Castilian
accent)*

KIT
I am Don Crithtoforo Rodrigo de Luna y
Thalamanca, Marquith of Theville and Grand
Counthilor to Hith Majesty Philip of Thpain.

SAVAGE
(Bowing low in wonder) Your Grace—

ROOKWOOD
*(Bowing low in wonder, speaking in unison with
SAVAGE)* Your Worshipfulness—

KIT
(Indicating WILL) And thith man ith my thpecial

agent in your landth. Hith name mutht remain a thecret, for hith own thafety.

WILL
Right. Now, you seek the woman you were molesting on the road, yes? *(He tosses KIT's satchel to ROOKWOOD)* Everything she had is in there. Search it if you like.

SAVAGE
Sir, if you please, where is the female now?

KIT
She no longer exitht. I mythelf ended her mitherable exithtenth. After taking my pleasure at leisure, of courth. She wath exthraordinarily, how you thay, dethirable.

SAVAGE
But then... why did you rescue her?

WILL
(As if speaking to an idiot) To prevent a scene, of course.

KIT
And to lull her into a fraudulent thense of thecuridad. Before she died, she condemnéd herthelf motht magnifithently.

ROOKWOOD
(Pulling KIT's wig from the satchel) What's this, then?

KIT
Imagine my dithtathte in dithrobing her and finding her to bear no hair upon her body!

HIGGINS
None at all?

KIT
None.

ROOKWOOD
(Under his breath) Fut that...

SAVAGE
Where's the paper?

ROOKWOOD
It's not here.

KIT
Papier? Do you thay papier?

SAVAGE
Yes, a paper!

KIT
A thingle sheet, with much writing? Why, we
thet it to the fire, of courth.

SAVAGE
(Approaching KIT in apparent rage) You set it to
the fire? *(Beat. He embraces KIT)* Praise God!

KIT
Now, my friendth, we mutht continue on our
way, delightful ath it hath been to thpeak with
you. If I could, though, athk you to refill my
purth...

SAVAGE
(Hand drifting again towards his knife) Why would
you need our money?

KIT
Alath, amigoth! Among my agenth many thins
ith the gamble, and he lotheth much money at
the horthe – he cannot rethitht a wager! Thilly,

thilly man! To bring the newth back to Thpain, I mutht have the fundingth. When you tell your mathterth the papier is dethtroyed, I am thertain they would not only approve, but altho repay... even if you were to, how you thay, exthaggerate how much you give to uth? Eh?

(KIT lays a finger aside his nose. SAVAGE does the same. Both laugh. SAVAGE hands over his purse and the CATHOLIC AGENTS depart)

KIT
How did you know that sign?

WILL
I know things.

KIT
Mmmmm... how lucky I am to have fallen in with a Papist heretic!

WILL
I'm not.

KIT
Oh, please say you are! It makes you that much more appealing!

WILL
My mother is – was – related to some.

KIT
Well, that's twice now I owe my life to you. Sadly, their masters won't be so credulous, and these rogues will be back on our trail before we know it. But soon we'll be in London with–

WILL
London?! I can't go to London!

KIT
Why not?

WILL
I... I...

KIT
Come on, out with it.

WILL
I'm a wanted man.

KIT
Delicious! O! You just keep getting better and better, don't you? What did you do?

WILL
I poached a deer from our Magistrate's estate, a tyrant named Lucy. Sir Thomas Lucy.

KIT
And he whipped you for it.

WILL
Aye, and he's not done with me. I can't go into society, Kit.

KIT
Never fear, my darling. We'll keep the lowest of low profiles in town, and when we deliver our message, you'll be pardoned of all past misdeeds.

WILL
Truly?

KIT
Her Majesty will not be stingy in terms of earthly rewards. A knighthood may be a trifle ambitious, but not out of the question. Surely, love, you have sussed out the treasure I possess.

WILL
Tell me if I've got this right: you disguised yourself as a serving wench, to serve a woman, someone important, and Catholic.

KIT
Indeed.

WILL
You ran off with one of her papers. Whatever's
on it is fatal to whoever carries it.

KIT
Indeed.

WILL
So, I'm asking myself... what woman lives in
Stafford, under guard, who would stand to gain
by treason and the restoration of the old faith to
England? And who do I come up with?

KIT
Pray tell.

WILL
Mary Stuart.

KIT
(Delightedly confirming his suspicion) Queen of
Scots.

WILL
Fut.

KIT
(Laying it on thick) Our nation's greatest foe.

WILL
Fut.

KIT
(Victorious) Queen Elizabeth's prisoner and focus
of all Catholic hopes in England!

WILL
Fut all!!

(Slight beat, then KIT can't help himself)

KIT
(A devious whisper) The ultimate evil...

WILL
Stop your mouth. And this paper you have
incriminates her?

KIT
Would you like to see it? *(He produces a small
paper from his sleeve and hands it to WILL)*

WILL
*(Reading from the start of two long lines of dense
text)* CFPXCFXSP... It just goes on like that...

KIT
It is, of course, in code.

WILL
What does it say?

KIT
Therein lies the sport; I have no earthly notion!
The Queen's code-breakers will tell us. Or
rather, they won't, but we'll be showered with
more gold than we could spend in a year.

WILL
Wait – you have no idea what this message
reads?

KIT
None!

WILL
Tell me I have not risked wrack and ruin, that
I have not run away for the second time in my
life, consorted with Catholics and murderers and
– and you! – all for what might be Mary Stuart's
request for fresh linens!

KIT
Think upon the degree to which they desire it
regained. It is not inconsequential. Come. Soon
we shall be in London, and our fortunes will be
forever changed!

*(The scene shifts to London. The CHORUS enters as
WILL and KIT enter the city)*

CHORUS
London: the faire that never ever ends! Let us
pause to savor our hero's first view of that glis-
tening conglomeration of ideas and intrigues. To
Will, the promise of London had always been as
seductive as that first glimpse of a Mysterious
Lady in the road. But as the Lady had shed her
guise, revealing both more and less beneath, so
too was the real London something less and something more than his fantasies. His first impres-
sion was not of grandeur, but of teeming squalor
and vice, a sheer press of humanity inspiring fear
and awe in equal measure.

*(WILL and KIT cross London Bridge amidst a great
press of people. As KIT crosses away to eye the wares
in a nearby stall, WILL stops short, looking up at
something the audience cannot see)*

CHORUS
And as he made his way across London Bridge,
Will was shaken from his grand thoughts by
something far darker.

WILL
(Aside) O!

CHORUS
The heads of traitors and scoundrels, mounted
in warning to would-be evil-doers. Though the
eyes were gone, taken for jelly by carrion birds,
one was familiar.

WILL
(Aside) Edward...?

CHORUS
Like the Triumphing generals of Rome, Will
heard a whisper in his ear, *'Respice te, hominem
te momento.'* "Look behind you," the city said...

WILL
(Aside) "Remember you are only a man."

(CHORUS exits)

KIT
(Taking note of WILL's horrified stare) Do you
know him?

WILL
Edward Arden. My mother's cousin. A good man.
Catholic, but good. All the Ardens are Catholic.

KIT
Which is how you knew the sign.

WILL
(Nodding) Cousin Edward helped a runaway

priest. Thomas Lucy found out. And captured
him. He's made quite a name for himself hunt-
ing Catholics. Bastard.

KIT
So you poached his deer.

WILL
Yes! And I was arrested. The bastard judge let
Lucy do the whipping with his own bastard
hand. A dozen lashes.

KIT
Well, fear not, my friend. Our fate will not be
that of these poor souls. Soon, this will all be
behind you.

WILL
Where are we headed?

KIT
Seething Lane.

WILL
Really? It couldn't be Tranquility Lane? The
Avenue of Warm Embraces?

KIT
No street in the shadow of the Tower of London
could have such a name.

(They approach an impressive stone abode)

WILL
What now?

KIT
We ask to see Sir Francis.

WILL
(With real trepidation) Francis Walsingham? The

Queen's spymaster? We're actually going to talk
to him?

KIT
That's right. Face to face. And Walsingham's
going to fix everything.

(KIT knocks on the door. PHELIPPES appears. He
is greatly displeased to see KIT)

PHELIPPES
Mr. Marlowe. You are meant to be in Paris.

KIT
Alas, Mr. Phelippes, Paris proved too dull! Will,
this is Phelippes – Walsingham's right hand and
an accomplished spy in his own right.

PHELIPPES
Why are you here?

KIT
I – we, that is – we come bearing a message for
Sir Francis. The rest I refuse to say where ears
can hear.

PHELIPPES
I don't have time for this.

KIT
I assure you: you do. (He whispers in PHELIPPES'
ear)

PHELIPPES
(Growing noticeably tense) You have this message?

KIT
I do, but I will place it only in Sir Francis' hand.

PHELIPPES
He is out.

KIT
Then we shall wait.

PHELIPPES
You shall not. Go to the Elephant, and stay there.
We'll send for you.

KIT
The Elephant? *(Pouting)* I prefer the Peacock.

PHELIPPES
The Elephant. You'll draw less attention.

KIT
We are a trifle out of purse to take rooms...

(PHELIPPES brusquely tosses a purse to KIT)

KIT
Many thanks! And tell Sir Francis this paper will
be the settling of all accounts.

(KIT and WILL bow and step away)

WILL
He didn't seem pleased.

KIT
He never does. *(Eyeing the purse)* But this is well!
Come, we're off to the Newington Butts! *(He
leads WILL through the streets)*

WILL
(Glancing around furtively) Shouldn't we go to the
Elephant and wait for the summons?

KIT
Pish. If they mean to keep us waiting, we'll do
the same to them. Besides, this coin isn't going
to spend itself.

WILL
You're taking me to an archery yard?

KIT
When the bow gave way to the musket, the yards were turned over for entertainments.

WILL
Bear baiting? Bulls?

KIT
I'd hardly term bear baiting 'entertainment', though the crowds lap it up like a dog does vomit. No, there's our destination!

(They come within sight of an octagonal building of nearly three stories, marked with flags and a sign - the Newington Butts)

WILL
'Tis a theatre! *(Reading the sign)* "The Spanish Tragedie: or Hieronymo is Mad Again."

KIT
(Continuing to read) "Containing the lamentable end of Don Horatio, and Bel-imperia; with the pitifull death of olde Hieronymo." Sounds juicy! I wonder who wrote it.

WILL
(Referencing the flags) Whose device is that?

KIT
These are the Earl of Oxford's men, a rogue called de Vere – always in some trouble or other with the Queen.

WILL
Never heard of him.

KIT
He doesn't matter. Come, let's hear this new play!

(They pass into the theatre, jostled by a great crowd)

WILL
How many people fit in here?

KIT
Over a thousand.

(The rear wall of the stage looks like a house supported by two great wooden pillars. Overhead is a roof like a temple, the underside of which is painted like the night sky, with astrological signs and sigils)

KIT
Up there, above the stage, are the Heavens. There's a trap door in the center; sometimes it opens and a man flies down on a rope. Deus ex machina. Can you imagine hanging from a slender thread so high?

WILL
No!

(There is a flourish of trumpets and two men enter: the ACTOR PLAYING THE GHOST OF ANDREA, dressed in a Spanish doublet, and the ACTOR PLAYING REVENGE, wearing a scarlet robe)

ACTOR PLAYING THE GHOST OF ANDREA
When this eternal substance of my soul
Did live imprisoned in my wanton flesh,
I was a Courtier in the Spanish Court.
My name was Don Andrea...

AUDIENCE MEMBER 1
Ooo! He's a ghost!

AUDIENCE MEMBER 2
Who's the other? Death?

ACTOR PLAYING THE GHOST OF ANDREA
Forthwith, Revenge, she rounded thee in th'
eare...

AUDIENCE MEMBER 3
He's Revenge!

ACTOR PLAYING THE GHOST OF ANDREA
And bad thee lead me through the gates of horn,
Where dreames have passage in the silent night.
No sooner had she spoke but we weere heere,
I wot not how, in the twinkling of an eye.

KIT
Oh, I know who wrote this! Thomas Kyd, the
lost little lamb!

ACTOR PLAYING REVENGE
Then know, Andrea, that thou ariv'd
Where thou shalt see the author of thy death...

*(The CHORUS enters as the play continues in
dumbshow)*

CHORUS
It was Will's first sight of actors giving life to
words upon a proper stage. He had seen players
in times past, as the travelling companies passed
through Stratford. But this—

WILL
(Aside) This must be what it was like in ancient
times, when Julius Caesar and Pompey the Great
took in a play.

CHORUS
The story turned on a father's grief over the

murder of his son, and his revenge upon the
murderers. It was hypnotically violent, and
the crowd was transfixed. The father turned to
murder, the mother to suicide. In the Fourth Act,
the grieving Hieronymo, lamenting the death of
his son, spoke these lines...

ACTOR PLAYING HIERONYMO
When I was young, I gave my mind
And plied myself to fruitless Poetry;
Which though it profit the professor naught,
Yet is it passing pleasing to the world.

CHORUS
And it was as though the playwright stepped
inside Will's skin and unearthed a golden kernel
of truth.

WILL
(Aside) Though it profit not, yet is Poetry pleasing to the world...

CHORUS
As the story neared its end, a trap was set for the
villain: the characters in the play staged a play
of their own, not revealing that the knives they
wielded were real.

WILL
(Aside) A play, within a play. Ingenious!

CHORUS
At the end, real cannons sounded, and as swiftly
as it had begun, it was over. Barely two midday
hours had passed. But something had awakened
in Will.

WILL
(Aside) This... This is... possible. I never knew...

(The CHORUS exits as the crowd roars its approval. KIT notices WILL's rapt expression)

KIT
Well?

WILL
That was simply marvelous. Who wrote it? Thomas Kyd, you said?

(WILL and KIT travel to the Elephant and Castle)

KIT
Aye. A good fellow, Thomas, but he's tied to an Earl, who demands he do actual work. He's a scrivener, using letters for profit, not Art. Yet the best Art comes from trying times, history tells us. And based on what we just saw, his times are extraordinarily trying.

WILL
You thought the play was good?

KIT
It was excellent. Too good for Thomas, in fact. Someone must have written it for him.

WILL
Take credit for another's work? I could never do that.

KIT
Come, let us revel in as fine a form as the poor Elephant will allow.

(They enter the Elephant, where an INNKEEPER is serving various layabouts)

INNKEEPER
(Not pleased to see him) Christopher Marlowe.

KIT
That's right – I have returned! Now, be a dear and
fetch us some wine. *(Sitting down with WILL)* So
tell me, sweet William, is not London a magnifi-
cent feast for the senses?

WILL
It is certainly more than I ever imagined.

KIT
London is woman in all her forms: loving mother,
devoted sister, knowing wife, sultry mistress, and
the toothless old hag who begs for coins. Only
all at once.

*(The INNKEEPER serves them cups of wine as
HUFFING KATE appears across the room)*

HUFFING KATE
(In a fury) Christopher Marlowe!

KIT
O God. Speaking of sultry hags, here's Huffing
Kate.

HUFFING KATE
(Approaching) You took my best gown, Christopher.

KIT
It was, and remains, a fine gown. That's what
made me have need of it.

HUFFING KATE
Gave it to some wench, did you?

KIT
I assure you, no other woman has worn it.

HUFFING KATE
A likely story!

WILL
And absolutely true.

KIT
Here, take my wine. Drink, and be friends, we shall make amends.

HUFFING KATE
'Tisn't burnt. I like my wine burnt, you know.

KIT
It shall be burnt. I know how to burn it, without fire.

HUFFING KATE
How?

KIT
Marry, thus. Take a seat, and then place this cup, with the greatest care, between your knees. In so fiery a place as that, the wine must be near scorched black!

(HUFFING KATE slaps KIT)

HUFFING KATE
O, that's done ye, Kit Marlowe! I'm fetching Blacke Davie! *(She downs her wine and storms off)*

KIT
Blacke Davie?!?!? Damnable cockatrice. Curséd shrew. She's an angry piece of flesh, Kate is.

(WILL catches sight of SAVAGE, ROOKWOOD, and HIGGINS entering the Elephant, hoods pulled over their heads, trying to look inconspicuous)

WILL
(Under his breath) Fut! Kit! Look! The Catholics have found us!

KIT
Fut!

WILL
What's their plan?

KIT
Nothing here. Too public. But if we bolt, they
run us down. If we stay, they outlast us.

WILL
What do we do?

KIT
What we need is... *(Hearing the sound of singing from the street)* Singing! A chorus of angels
could not sound sweeter. Salvation lies in the
fool, Will, always in the fool!

*(TARLTON enters. He wears a sword on his hip and
sings loudly, playing a lute)*

TARLTON
(Singing)
COME THOU MONARCH OF THE VINE,
PLUMPIE BACCHUS, WITH PINK EYNE:
IN THY VATS OUR CARES BE DROWN'D,
WITH THY GRAPES OUR HAIRS BE CROWN'D.
CUP US TILL THE WORLD GO ROUND,
CUP US TILL THE WORLD GO ROUND!

KIT
Tarlton! Join us, won't you?

TARLTON
Tarlton is no carpenter, to join mismatched pairs.

KIT
Will my purse purchase your fellowship?

TARLTON
(Sitting with them) Depends how deep your purse
reaches.

KIT
For you, to the depths of Tartarus... which is
where you belong! This is my friend Will Falstaff.

TARLTON
Dick Tarlton. Forgive me if I don't make a leg,
but I don't think I could rise again. I was supping
at Court, and was mightily overserved.

WILL
At Court?

KIT
Maestro Tarlton here is Queen Elizabeth's favorite fool.

TARLTON
Or so she says. There are many idiots she favors:
the porky Bacon, the stalwart Stanley, to say
nothing of the devious de Vere. But 'tis me they
call fool; and perhaps I am, as they profit by
their foolishness, while I sew patches in my hose.
(Reaching for KIT's cup) Give me some wine.

KIT
(Pulling his cup away) But my dear Spotted Dick,
there is a price for wetting your lips.

TARLTON
When is there not?

KIT
We are in peril, and require aid. There are three
men in this room who wish us ill.

TARLTON
Far more than three, Marlowe, I assure you.

KIT
(Leaning in close) Listen – I'm on business from
the Queen.

TARLTON, KIT & WILL
Long may she reign.

TARLTON
Say no more. Do you wish their arrest, or your
escape?

KIT
The latter will suffice. We don't know who to
trust at present.

TARLTON
Who now is the fool?

WILL
At the moment, sir, the fool is we. We must turn
the tables, and make the fool he.

*(WILL nods towards SAVAGE. SAVAGE removes
his hood in a menacing fashion)*

TARLTON
I see why you fear him. What d'ye know of him?

KIT
His name is John Savage, a Catholic in the service
of Mary of Scotland.

TARLTON
Dun's the mouse! Well, well; let me see... *(He
briefly furrows his brow, then rises as an idea dawns)* I
think it best we have all the players on the board.
(Calling across the room) Savage? John Savage! By

God, Kit, do you see? It's John Savage! Savage, come and join us!

KIT

What, Rookwood? Are you here, too? Come and crush a cup, Master Rookwood!

(When it becomes clear that KIT and TARLTON won't stop shouting their names, SAVAGE, ROOKWOOD, and HIGGINS approach. TARLTON stares openly at SAVAGE's nose)

SAVAGE

(In a low whisper) You're dead men.

TARLTON

(Loudly) Marlowe, our good friend Savage says we're dead men.

KIT

(Loudly) That doesn't sound like the huggable John Savage I know...

SAVAGE

No more names!

ROOKWOOD

(To KIT, accusingly) You're not Spanish!

KIT

Alas, the span of my Spanishness has been spent.

SAVAGE

Fellow, our quarrel is with these two men. Clear off, and leave this pair to us.

TARLTON

(Indignant) You mean I'm not the center of your world? I refuse to believe it! I am Dick Tarlton! I am the Queen's own Fool! *(He performs a fancy*

feat of tumbling or acrobatics) You really have no use for me?

SAVAGE
None.

TARLTON
(Bringing his right hand up in a slow and deliberate gesture) The fico for thee, then.

(SAVAGE gasps and places his hand on his sword hilt. The others follow suit. The tension holds briefly, then is broken by the door slamming open as BLACKE DAVIE enters, followed by HUFFING KATE)

Blacke Davie
MAAAARLOOOOWE!!!

WILL
Blacke Davie, I presume?

TARLTON
(Smiling broadly) Perfect.

HUFFING KATE
Kit Marlowe! You've got a date with Blacke Davie's fist!

TARLTON
Say, Kate, lend us a hand, would you?

KIT
What can she do? *(Setting up TARLTON)* She can't seduce three men at once.

TARLTON
You think not? A cohort of men can parade her nethers. I should know...

(HUFFING KATE yowls and charges at TARLTON, who deftly avoids, causing her to land

*headfirst in KIT's lap. Not missing a beat, KIT
grabs her by the waist and hauls her heels-over-head,
exposing her smallclothes. BLACKE DAVIE roars,
draws his sword, and stabs at KIT, but TARLTON
deftly parries the blow, causing it to nearly strike
SAVAGE. SAVAGE draws. Everyone draws)*

SAVAGE
(To BLACKE DAVIE) You dare?!

INNKEEPER
(Delicately inserting himself) Friends. Let's not get
carried away...

*(TARLTON hands his lute over to the
INNKEEPER, who accepts it with resignation,
knowing exactly what this means)*

TARLTON
Oh, Davie! *(Points to Catholics)* These men have
all tried Kate's virtue, too - and found it want-
ing!

BLACKE DAVIE
Raaaaaaaarrrrrgggggghhh!!!

*(A massive melee ensues. BLACK DAVIE tries
to pummel KIT and kill the CATHOLICS.
The CATHOLICS try to kill KIT and WILL.
TARLTON sews mischief and defends KIT and
WILL. HUFFING KATE goes after KIT and
TARLTON. The INNKEEPER endeavors to save
his cups, benches, and other property from excess
damage. Both the INNKEEPER and TARLTON
protect the lute. KIT deftly dodges the flying blades
and pulls WILL to the door)*

KIT
(To WILL) Go, go, go!

(They exit the Elephant and run through the streets. They hear a crash and tumult behind them)

WILL
What about Tarlton?

KIT
He'll handle Davie. O fut! The Catholics are chasing us.

(WILL looks back and sees that SAVAGE and ROOKWOOD are in pursuit. The four race through the streets of London in an epic chase sequence)

KIT
Turn right!

WILL
They're closing!

KIT
Left! Right again! A sangre! A fuego! A sacco!

WILL
Where are we going?

KIT
Away from them!

WILL
We're going to run out of city!

KIT
We're in London! *(Running down an alley, they pass several doors. After several attempts, KIT finds an unlocked door)* See! Perfect! It's a door! Opportunity presents!

WILL
But where does it go?

KIT
I don't know. Safety and freedom!

(KIT pushes WILL through the door and they find themselves at the bottom of an enclosed pit with high walls. They hear the roar of a great crowd)

CROWD
Orsino! Orsino! Orsino!

WILL
What in the name of—

(They turn back to the door through which they entered just as SAVAGE and ROOKWOOD burst in)

SAVAGE
(To ROOKWOOD) Get them!

(They run another direction and an enormous snarling bear comes into view, tied to a stake by a rope)

KIT & WILL
Bear-baiting!

KIT
(To WILL) Well, my dear, out of the smoke and into the smother!

(The theatre erupts in chaos. SAVAGE and ROOKWOOD try to kill WILL and KIT. The bear attacks all four while roaring with rage. The crowd roars with excitement and terror)

KIT
(To WILL) Feeling baited?

WILL
(To KIT) I wish his claws were bated.

KIT
(To WILL) *So as to abate your fate.*

WILL
(To KIT) Now you're baiting me.

KIT
(To WILL) I'm a master of it!

SAVAGE
(To ROOKWOOD) Circle around! That way!

ROOKWOOD
(To SAVAGE) Fut that!

(The bear rakes SAVAGE across the arm. SAVAGE punches the bear in the face, causing it to collapse)

SAVAGE
(To ROOKWOOD) Now, get them!

(The bear revives and rears up on its hind legs in rage. The crowd goes wild)

WILL
(To KIT) What now?

KIT
(To WILL, unbuttoning his jerkin) Get ready!

WILL
(To KIT) For what?!?!

(KIT runs behind the bear and launches himself onto its back. The bear roars and swats as KIT wraps his jerkin around the beast's head, blinding it)

KIT
Now, Will! Cut the rope!

(WILL tumbles past the bear and cuts the rope securing it. The crowd screams. KIT leaps from the bear's

back to the top of the wall enclosing the pit. SAVAGE and ROOKWOOD exit pursued by the bear)

WILL
(Watching the exit-pursued-by-bear) Fantastic.

(KIT helps WILL out of the pit and they slip out the theatre into a nearby alley)

KIT
Well, I fear the Elephant has closed itself to our trunks.

WILL
How on earth did they know where we were?

KIT
We were betrayed.

WILL
By whom?

KIT
There is but one choice. Which means we have an added value to present Sir Francis: the word of a traitor on his staff. Let's go.

WILL
Where?

KIT
I know a place...

(Later that evening, WILL and KIT lurk outside of a fashionable building. A storm is approaching in the distance. PHELIPPES emerges and takes a pinch of snuff)

WILL
(Whispering) Ah! Our traitor.

KIT
Mr. Phelippes likes the odd game of chance,
you see. But working for the Queen's spymaster,
he can't indulge himself openly. So Sir Francis
arranged this gambling den for men who mustn't
be compromised.

(PHELIPPES passes; KIT and WILL trail him)

WILL
What's the plan?

KIT
There's a secret entrance, I'm sure, to
Walsingham's lair. When he gets there, we
improvise.

(PHELIPPES ducks into a narrow alley)

KIT
Aha. I was right. Seething Lane is just around the
corner. This must be a back way in!

*(PHELIPPES produces a key and unlocks an unre-
markable door. KIT takes WILL's sword, sneaks
up behind the spy and places the blade to his neck.
Thunder rumbles)*

KIT
Hello, dearie.

PHELIPPES
(With disdain) Christopher Marlowe.

KIT
Ah, ah! Not a sound. Now, as you know, we
carry urgent news regarding a plot against Her
Majesty. This news must reach the ears of Sir
Francis. Take us to him.

(PHELIPPES leads them into the building. They come to a door. PHELIPPES nods. KIT knocks)

WALSINGHAM
(From within) Come.

(They enter a study. WALSINGHAM sits at a desk, dressed in black, poring over papers by candlelight)

PHELIPPES
Sir Francis, forgive me. Marlowe waylaid me on my entrance.

WALSINGHAM
(To KIT) You went unobserved, I trust.

KIT
(Genuinely obedient) Yes, my lord.

WALSINGHAM
Very well. Release him. *(As KIT does so)* Phelippes, tell the Marchioness that our meeting must be postponed. Then return and stay close.

(PHELIPPES bows and exits. Lightning strikes)

WALSINGHAM
So, Marlowe. You abandoned your post in France. You know what this means.

KIT
Nothing short of utter disgrace. Unless I have something of greater value than seducing young Parisian secretaries for you.

WALSINGHAM
Who is your companion?

KIT
Will Falstaff here had the misfortune to save

my life, and then assisted me in my quest to bring you the thing you crave most in all the world.

WALSINGHAM
An end to the Spanish?

KIT
An end to Mary Stuart.

(Lightning strikes. WALSINGHAM holds out his hand. KIT hands him the paper)

KIT
It's from Mary herself. She sneaks out messages out of confinement through the bung of her ale-casks, you see, and this is one of them. It's in code, naturally, but I'm sure you can deal with such trifles.

(WALSINGHAM rises and frowns at the missive. He crosses to his candle to better read it)

KIT
We tried to deliver it earlier. We left a message with Phelippes and he explicitly told us to wait at the Elephant. Oddly enough, we'd hardly sat down at the Elephant when we were attacked by Mary's men. I'm afeared, my lord, you have a traitor here.

WALSINGHAM
Are there any copies?

KIT
None! I know my business, my lord.

WALSINGHAM
Forgive me, I had to ask. *(He sets the paper alight)*

KIT
(Horrified) What are you doing?!

WALSINGHAM
Christopher Marlowe, you are the king of fools.
Do you think that you, in your wig and false
bosoms, could discover a truth hidden from this
office? From me?

KIT
You already knew?

WALSINGHAM
Of course we knew. And do you think that
Phelippes can do anything without my know-
ing? It was not he who set the Papists upon you.
'Twas I.

KIT
No.

WALSINGHAM
I hoped they might deal with you before you
reached this office. That they failed to do so is -
disappointing.

KIT
My Lord, I don't underst–

WALSINGHAM
We own the brewer! We receive every message
Mary sends out! It was quite a trial, engineering
a method for her to send treasonous communi-
cations without her suspecting us. Yes! You see it
now. Rather than do us a service, your idiotic lark
has risked an operation that took months to put
in place. This is why professionals obey orders.
Instead, by playing the hero, you've damaged the

nation, and quite possibly imperiled the throne.

KIT
That message—

WALSINGHAM
Whatever was in it, I assure you, we've already
seen and dealt with it. And now, alas, we must
deal with you. Phelippes!

(PHELLIPES enters with a SOLDIER)

WALSINGHAM
Take these two and have them killed.

WILL
Wait – what?

WALSINGHAM
It must seem accidental. And put a paper on
Marlowe that is smudged beyond recognition,
preferably by his own blood.

*(Lightning strikes. PHELLIPES and the SOLDIER
approach. KIT stands numb, crushed beyond belief)*

WILL
Kit?

KIT
I don't believe it.

WILL
Do something!

KIT
My inspiration has expired...

WILL
Kit!

WALSINGHAM
Take him away.

(With PHELLIPES focused on KIT, WILL sees an opening and pulls PHELLIPES' sword from his belt. He slashes wildly, forcing PHELLIPES back)

WILL
Come on, Kit, you bastard, stir yourself!

(The SOLDIER goes to draw, but WILL slashes at his hand, forcing him backwards)

KIT
What do I do?

WILL
I don't know! Improvise! *(Getting an idea)* The candle!

(KIT douses the candle. Darkness fills the room. There is the sound of swords slashing, yelps of pain, and bone-crunching thumps. Lightning sporadically illuminates dramatic moments of combat)

KIT
(In the darkness) What now? We need a way out!

WALSINGHAM
(In the darkness) Stop them!

WILL
(In the darkness) The window, Kit!

(There is the sound of a window shattering)

WALSINGHAM
(In the darkness) Marlowe!

WILL
(In the darkness) Jump!

(WILL and KIT yell as they throw themselves into the night. The scene shifts to the street in front of the house as WILL and KIT land hard, tumbling to break their fall. An alarm sounds)

WILL
What happened to you up there?

KIT
I don't understand. I always win. It's what makes being me so satisfying.

WILL
If we survive this, I'm going to punch you so hard.

KIT
If you devise a way for us to survive, you may do so and welcome!

(Cries rouse up all around them. A pistol shot explodes in the night, shattering part of a nearby wall)

WILL & KIT
Aaaaaaa!

(SOLDIERS appear from all directions armed with swords and hackbuts. A closed carriage with a DRIVER speeds towards them on the cobblestone street)

WILL
Look, Kit, a carriage!

(WILL and KIT leap aboard the carriage)

WILL
Take down the driver!

KIT
(Hurling the DRIVER to the street) Sorry!

WILL
Go on! Get this coach moving!

(KIT takes the reins as WILL fends off multiple SOLDIERS, one of whom makes it to the top of the carriage. He and WILL face off atop the speeding carriage, ducking multiple gunshots)

WILL
(To the SOLIDER) Are we really doing this?

(The SOLDIER attacks. As they fight, KIT makes a particularly sharp turn)

KIT
Hold on!

(WILL and the SOLDIER duel till WILL manages to kick him off the top of the carriage)

KIT
Where are we going?

WILL
I don't know! You tell me! Out of the city, right?

KIT
There's no way out of the city that doesn't mean passing through a gate. And at this time of night—

WILL
Watch the road!

WILL & KIT
Dog!

(KIT pulls the horses sharply to one side to avoid a dog in the street. There is the scream of a woman from within the carriage)

KIT
Any idea who's inside?

WILL
Yes, I stopped and chatted her up.

KIT
The way tonight is progressing, I wouldn't be
surprised to find that we've abducted the Queen
herself.

(They both freeze)

WILL
You don't think...

KIT
(Looking back at WILL) No, it can't be...

HELENA
(From inside the carriage) I can hear you, you
know.

(WILL and KIT look at each other, then speak in
low whispers)

WILL
Not the Queen, right?

KIT
Too young. Definitely not the Queen. Will, you
need to go down there and convince our guest
to aid us.

WILL
Aid us?

KIT
We will never get through the gates if she
doesn't.

HELENA
(From inside the carriage) Are you highwaymen?
Are London robbers grown so bold?

WILL
We have no intent to molest you in any way. We
are gentlemen.

KIT
(With a smile) Speak for yourself.

HELENA
(From inside the carriage) Prove it.

WILL
(Lowering his sword into the carriage) Now, may I
please come down and speak with you?

HELENA
(From inside the carriage) Enter.

*(HELENA opens the door. WILL lowers himself
inside, finding a regal woman dressed for court with
ruff and jewelry and a breathtaking dress. She puts
WILL on point with his own sword)*

WILL
Hello.

HELENA
No sudden moves, young man.

WILL
I am Will Falstaff. Whom do I have the honor to
address?

HELENA
My name is Helena.

KIT
Time, William, time!

WILL
Lady Helena, my friend and I are in terrible
danger. Through patriotic actions and no malice
in the world, we find ourselves chased by both
our nation's enemies and its defenders.

HELENA
Unfortunate.

WILL
Agreed. We seek only to go to earth until we can
prove our innocence.

HELENA
What, then, do you wish of me?

WILL
If you can pass us through the gates, we'll leave
your presence as quickly as we came.

HELENA
(Calling up to KIT) You there! Driver! What is
the nearest portal?

KIT
Cripplegate, my lady.

HELENA
Take us through.

WILL
Your ladyship, I cannot thank you enough.

HELENA
No. You cannot.

(KIT drives the carriage to Cripplegate, where three
GUARDS stand at the ready)

CRIPPLEGATE GUARD 1
Halt! Who's within?

KIT
A lady.

CRIPPLEGATE GUARD 2
(Wrenching the carriage door open) Out! All of you!

HELENA
How dare you? Can you not see the seal on the door?

CRIPPLEGATE GUARD 2
(Looking at the seal) Pardon us, your Ladyship. But at this hour—

HELENA
Does the hour excuse rudeness? Insolence?

CRIPPLEGATE GUARD 3
It's our commission to ask the names of any who pass in and out after daylight hours.

HELENA
Had you but asked, I'd have answered that I am Helena of Snakenborg, Marchioness of Northampton, Lady-in-Waiting to her Majesty the Queen. These are my servants.

WILL
Hello. I'm a servant.

CRIPPLEGATE GUARD 1
Begging your pardon, my lady. We'll open the gates at once. *(Calling off)* Open the gate!

(The gate opens, and KIT drives the carriage through)

HELENA
So, I presume your trouble stems from Sir Francis?

WILL
Ah. Yes. There was a... a misunderstanding.

HELENA
That happens often with Sir Francis.

WILL
I hope we haven't imperiled you.

HELENA
You're sweet, for kidnappers. *(As KIT slows the carriage)* Why are we stopping?

KIT
We're outside the walls.

(WILL and KIT disembark. HELENA follows, carrying WILL's sword)

WILL
Once again, you have our eternal gratitude. We'll leave you now and trouble you no more.

HELENA
Will you leave me stranded here, alone and help-less?

WILL
My lady—

HELENA
I jest. I'm more than capable of driving my own carriage. And I'm hardly defenseless... *(She performs a complicated invitation with WILL's sword)*

WILL
I can see that.

HELENA
My husband keeps a home in Whitefriars, which

is not far off. I'm staying there while he's in town for his knighting. Will you not join me for shelter? A meal? And a bed?

WILL
They'll trace us there, and put you in danger.

HELENA
And you don't know how far to trust me.

WILL
Thank you for helping us, my lady.

HELENA
"Be not forgetful to entertain strangers: for thereby have some entertained angels unawares." I'd like to know how your misadventure ends – so long as it ends well. I don't care for Tragic tales. There's too much real tragedy in the world.

(HELENA tosses WILL his sword, mounts her carriage and drives away)

KIT
Why, there's a wench.

WILL
Indeed. (Pause) Oh, Kit?

KIT
Yes?

(WILL sucker punches KIT)

WILL
Sorry.

KIT
No, I said you could. And I had it coming. I promised you riches and renown, but I've deliv-

ered only trial and tribulation. You must despise
me. Not that I blame you. I expect you'll be
parting ways with me now...

WILL
Kit Marlowe, waxing maudlin?

KIT
I ruined everything! O! If only I'd copied the
note! I see it curling into ashes before my
eyes. With that note we might have stood a
chance! Decipher it and figure out Mary's plot
ourselves!

WILL
If that is our sole obstacle, you may consider it
solved.

KIT
You copied it? But when?

WILL
No. I memorized it.

KIT
(Highly dubious) You memorized it.

WILL
(Closing his eyes, he takes a breath and then recites)
CFPXCFXSPBCTPW... Need I continue?

KIT
What! How? You saw it for all of ten seconds!

WILL
I have an exceptional memory. A gift from my
grandmother. Besides, in Lancashire there was
naught to do but memorize verses. And the more
a gift is used, the more it strengthens.

KIT
Does this mean you're sticking with me?

WILL
Listen, I don't know how this thing ends, but I'm going to see it through. Before I met you, I had no future. I couldn't even imagine a future. But you've brought me back from the dead. I thought I was... this one thing, but maybe I'm not.

(KIT kisses WILL. WILL responds)

KIT
My dearest darling William, you are full of surprises!

(KIT kisses WILL again. Lights out)

END OF ACT ONE

ACT II
THE PLAY'S THE THING

*(Lights rise on WILL and KIT in a London alleyway
early the next evening. WILL sits alone, contemplat-
ing his fate. KIT relieves himself against a nearby
wall)*

CHORUS
Imagine now the underbelly of London, those
dank byways where the watch never walks,
where madmen muster, and criminals hold court.
Here we find the subjects of our watch: would-
be heroes reduced to wanted men. Having only
narrowly escaped London, they were forced to
return, merging with the bustle at Bishopsgate.
Surrounded by the hum and clatter of the city,
with watchful eyes round every corner, they drew
carefully closer to the center of town, where they
waited for night to fall. For Will, paused here
amongst the filth and the offal, it was a moment
of reflection. On times past, and times yet to
come. Ever since his father's troubles began, Will

had lived only in response and reaction.

WILL
(Aside) Covering for his mistakes. Cleaning up
his messes.

CHORUS
Never before had he lived a life of action –
examining what he wanted, charting a destiny
separate from his father's ambitions.

WILL
(Aside) Dare I have my own desires? Dare I dream
of being more than I am?

CHORUS
But there was no–

WILL
(Aside) There is no Philosopher's Stone to turn
my lead into gold. I see that now. *(He steps forward
and takes the place of the CHORUS)* Stratford is
behind me. Lancashire is behind me. My days
of waiting and hiding are over. If there is to
be greatness in my future, I must perform the
alchemy myself.

*(The CHORUS nods and graciously exits as a cry
comes from deeper in the alley)*

POOR TOM
(Offstage) Fathom and a half! Come, snulbug,
Poor Tom'll feed ye!

WILL
Who's there?

KIT
(Doing up his breeches) Hush! Bedlam lies near

Bishopsgate, and sometimes they allow the lesser mads to wander, begging in the streets. Poor Toms, all.

("POOR TOM" enters: a ragged, twisted beggar. KIT pulls WILL aside to let him pass)

POOR TOM
Who's there! Who's there, poor Tom?

("POOR TOM" exits. During the following, assorted low-lifes pass through the area as KIT and WILL endeavor to remain inconspicuous)

WILL
All right, so our mission now is to uncypher the code. The time's come for you to be glass-clear. No more secrets. Tell me exactly how you came to possess the note.

KIT
In France, I was tasked with gaining the confidence of men of certain... predilections. One was a disgraced priest named Gilbert Gifford. I made short work of him, but then he was sent to England to serve Mary of Scots. I told my masters, but to my astonishment nothing came of it! So, I came to London in secret, borrowed Huffing Kate's best dress, and reunited with Gifford. Between fits of passion, we concocted a plan to place me in Mary's household. I told him I'd protect her from harm and be Gifford's eyes and ears in the castle. And it worked – they accepted me as a scullery maid. Soon, I sussed out the trick with the beer-kegs.

WILL
How does it work?

KIT
Mary has two secretaries allowed to her: one
French, one English. She dictates her message to
the one, who translates it into English, then the
English one puts it in code and seals it in the
bung of an empty beer barrel.

WILL
So how did you get the note?

KIT
I found it in Gifford's bag. After we—

WILL
Now, wait. That's not the route you just described.
Mary, to the French secretary, to the English
secretary to the barrel... Why would Gifford
have a note?

KIT
I thought they were just bypassing the system
out of convenience. But I guess... *(A revelation)* I
guess I don't know for certain. Maybe this proves
that it's a message Sir Francis hasn't seen!

WILL
All the more reason to get it deciphered. Come
on, you know London. Who here can help us
break the code?

KIT
(Smiling) Ah! We must seek out those notori-
ous fiends, those men of no standing. We want
lithe Lyly, wily Watson, and the great Greene —
in short, we want the Wits!

*(The scene changes to the White Hart Inn, where the
room is thick with tobacco smoke and ruffians. LYLY,*

GREENE, and EM BALL drink at a table. EM sits on GREENE's lap. KIT and WILL enter)

KIT
Where the devil is my drink?!

LYLY
Quick, it's Marlowe – hide your wit, lest he steal it.

GREENE
The great walking spur, that makes a jangling noise but never pricks!

KIT
O, that I could see the brains that coined such a jest, that I might hug them, you fat-kidney'd rascal. *(He embraces both men heartily)* Where's Watson?

GREENE
He was in a foul mood, and decided to lighten it by stepping out to hear his fellow members of the bar engage in low matters.

KIT
You mean matters of law.

GREENE
I know what I mean, and say what I know.

EM
But rarely know what you say.

LYLY
Or pay what you owe.

KIT
This is Will. Will, John Lyly. Lyly's written a number of books you may have read. Folks heap

them with praise, but I can't stomach them,
myself. And speaking of stomachs, this is the
great – and I mean great – Robert Greene, who
like me is a man of discernment and culture –
meaning he hails from Cambridge. Poor, sad John
here rose from the stews of Oxford.

GREENE
I actually studied at both, so I'm twice the man
they are.

EM
(Patting GREENE's belly) Only twice? You mean
thrice at least.

GREENE
'Tis only fitting that in girth I try to match my
genius.

EM
(To WILL) I'm Emily. They call themselves "wits,"
but I'm the only one with any sense around here.

KIT
Truth is truth.

LYLY
A pity you weren't here yesterday, Marlowe. We
were taking to pieces that new, dare I call it,
"play" that Thomas Kyd fashioned at the Butts.

KIT
The Spanish Tragedie? We saw it.

WILL
And liked it.

GREENE
Predictably.

WILL
Meaning?

GREENE
That blood-soaked mess was designed to appeal
to the masses. Thomas Kyd!

EM
Here we go…

GREENE
How dare he – a mere scrivener, a copyist, a
clerk! – set himself among the ranks of educated
men?

LYLY
Truly, he has not fed of the dainties bred in the
hallowed halls of learning.

GREENE
Aye! That's why he's so lean. He has not eaten
paper, as it were. He has not drunk ink! He is an
animal, only sensible in the duller parts.

LYLY
He would do well to study – nay, to emulate –
the works of his betters.

EM
Oh, please. I saw Sapho and Phao.

WILL
And what is it that offends you more? That he
dared to write a play? Or that it's so popular?
Yesterday, I witnessed a thousand people thrill-
ing to the words being spoken on that stage. His
words summoned spirits and brought the mighty
low. What have your words done today?

EM
Mostly gotten him slapped.

GREENE
And who are you to address me so? What
University did you say you hailed from?

WILL
The University of the universe, with providence
my professors and my opinions my own.

GREENE
Ha! Not a University man. I knew you at once.
(He belches in WILL's face) Little bull's pizzle.

WILL
Massive tallow-catch.

(KIT and LYLY are mildly shocked. EM chuckles)

GREENE
Will you turn your knavery upon a gentleman
and clout the air with petty insults?

WILL
Would they were less petty, that my knave's clouts
could fan the air of the gentleman's ungentle
breath.

GREENE
You argue like an infant; go whip your gig.

WILL
Lend me your horn to make one and I'll whip
you about circum circa! *(He spins GREENE
around and makes the horns as the others laugh)*
Behold! A gig of cuckhold's horn.

GREENE
(Roaring himself purple in the face) You little upstart

crow! You mizzling, pizzling, untutored, unlettered, puny insult to the very idea of manhood!

WILL

You upended Elephant! You grizzling, fizzling, unmannered, unsobered, horse-collapsing insult to the very idea of humanity!

(For a moment, all is deathly still. GREENE looks like a cannon, about to explode. Then suddenly he bursts into laughter, howling with delight. EM and LYLY join him)

GREENE
Well done, lad.

KIT
Enough. To the purpose. My friends, we have a coded message from Mary Stuart that must be deciphered to save us. And the Queen.

KIT, WILL, LYLY, GREENE & EM
Long may she reign.

LYLY
And thus you come to the Wits.

GREENE
(With a sideways look at WILL) My wits are sodden and useless, as has been mentioned. I doubt I have the sense to make sense of anything.

EM
(Comforting him with a kiss) Yet still you must try.

(KIT gives WILL a tray of paper, a pen, and a bottle of ink. WILL closes his eyes for a moment and then sets down a long string of letters on a piece of paper)

LYLY
No breaks between words? Pity. But I suppose that's part of the cipher. First we should note frequency. I believe E is the most common letter in the English language.

WILL
How many double letters are there in English? I see four paired Ns, and one WW.

LYLY
Could be double letters, or two words butted together. Well, given frequency of use, it's likely that either C or N represent E. I propose we first attempt a simple transposition method. Kit, you and Greene take C, see what comes of it. Will, join me in an N.

(They work for a moment)

GREENE
Gibberish.

WILL
What's the most common letter after E?

GREENE
Who can say? By whose spelling? Damn! I wish we could agree on a formalized spelling for English – it makes this so much harder! Garbage language...

LYLY
Now, now. English is a proper tongue, fit for proper discourse.

GREENE
It's a boorish tongue, livened only by adoptions from Latin, Greek, and–

LYLY
Don't say it!

GREENE
French.

LYLY
(Under his breath) I hate the French so much...

KIT
Don't forget Spanish and Italian. We are indiscriminate stealers of tongues.

GREENE
Thieves of words, aye. Our own tongue can't express lofty thoughts without them. There's a reason men of learning use foreign phrases to debate grand ideas. English is unsuited to high talk.

KIT
Why write plays in our native tongue, then, if it's so vile?

GREENE
It's where the coins are – grubby common coins from grubby common men.

WILL
Do you know why English is on the rise?

GREENE
O! This will be good.

WILL
I think it's a mark of independence. Latin is the tongue of the Pope, but English is the language of protest. We've broken free from the moorings of the past, and set sail to our own North Star.

GREENE
How can we be independent from that which
gives us life? Aristotle, Plato, Ovid? They are the
North Stars of poetry. Cut ties with them and
we are adrift!

WILL
Dante made his great poem in De Vulgari
Eloquentia – the eloquent vulgarity of his native
tongue.

GREENE
Eloquence is lost on the vulgar.

EM
Says the man who consorts with vagabonds.

WILL
The world is changing. English will soon become
the new lingua franca.

GREENE
Bah!

WILL
It will. *(Finding the argument in the moment)*
And not in spite of its gutterly bastardization
– because of it. We adapt, we grow. So too does
our tongue. Yes, we are the beneficiaries of all
that has gone before. But what new Latin words
are there? Greek, Italian, French – they're all
codified, they have no flex, no urgency. English
is a living tongue, and young! We don't yet have
all the words, but we will! Only when English
ceases to grow, when it is stifled by rules and
strictures, will it die!

*(KIT, LYLY, and EM break into spontaneous
applause. GREENE begrudgingly joins them)*

GREENE
Very well. But you may lament the lack of codi-
fication. Such strictures would aid us in defeat-
ing your blasted cypher!

LYLY
'Tis no use. The substitution must random. An
encoder has a sheet with all the letters matched
to their disguise, and the uncoder has its twin.
We'll never break it but by chance.

WILL
Then we must place our hands upon the key
itself.

KIT
Gifford had the note, so chances are good he's
got one. We can start by searching his rooms.

EM
And what if he catches you? Better to follow
him, see who he contacts.

WILL
Yes! One of his Catholic allies might also have
a key.

KIT
Excellent notion! *(To WILL)* Let's go.

WILL
Not you.

KIT
Why not?

WILL
He knows you, both as man and girl. Far better
that I do it.

KIT
You're not a Londoner, you have no idea how to blend in.

EM
Boys. This is clearly a job for my brother.

KIT, LYLY & GREENE
(Delighted at the notion) Cutting Ball!

GREENE
O, marvelous! You two get some rest while we go hunt him down. You can use my room upstairs to stay out of sight. Your work begins tomorrow!

(WILL and KIT cross to Greene's rooms and flop down on the floor)

KIT
So, tell me, sweetling, what was that with Greene? Are you biased against the portly slobberers of the world?

WILL
I misliked his manner.

KIT
That's no answer. Come. No more secrets, remember? Why did you engage him so ardently?

WILL
Because the more he railed against common language and common men... the more I saw in him the cause of all my troubles.

KIT
Thomas Lucy?

WILL
No. My father. All my life, he thought himself

better than – better than our neighbors, our whole town. His one passion was to bear a coat of arms. A tanner! He even crafted a sign for himself.

KIT
And then...?

WILL
Then he fell into his cups and the family purse unraveled.

KIT
A familiar tale.

WILL
Aye. But all of Stratford urged him on, because eyeball afloat in wine, my father was a man of wit and humor: the lord of the tavern, the earl of the alehouse. Until he had to be carted home, a common laughingstock. Everything he had, everything he'd dreamed of – he pissed it all away. Because in the end, he... *(A discovery)* he didn't deserve it.

KIT
Well, Greene isn't your father. And neither are you. Forget the past. The past is prologue.

WILL
Our history defines us.

KIT
We define ourselves. In word and deed. In the moment. *(He leans in to kiss WILL, but WILL pulls away)* Last night...

WILL
Last night was a mistake.

KIT
A mistake?

WILL
I don't mean a mistake. It's just the timing. We have the Sword of Damocles hanging over our heads, Kit. Until we're free...

KIT
What are you afraid of? *(When WILL doesn't answer)* As you wish. When you're ready, you know where to find me. *(He blows WILL a kiss and lies down to sleep)*

WILL
(Aside) What am I afraid of? I inherited much from my father. I have his nose, his hair, his eyes... And there's the rub! If I have his eyes, what if I'm just as blind? He ruined every relationship he ever had, and never saw it coming. He was always overreaching, grasping for what he never deserved. His pride runs strong in my blood. What if I'm no more worthy of greatness – or of happiness – than my father?

(The next morning, GREENE enters with CUTTING BALL, who is dressed like a filthy beggar. He carries a sack over his shoulder)

KIT
Cutting Ball! Well met.

CUTTING BALL
(Not delighted to see him) Marlowe.

GREENE
Allow me to present Cutting Ball, the true Hades of London, commander of a rowsey rabblement of rakehells. Cutting Ball, Will Falstaff.

(GREENE gives CUTTING BALL a significant look and exits. CUTTING BALL pulls another set of filthy, ragged clothes from his sack and tosses them to WILL)

CUTTING BALL
Put 'em on, Falstaff.

WILL
(Examining the disgusting clothing) Who did they belong to previously?

CUTTING BALL
A corpse.

WILL
Whose corpse?

CUTTING BALL
Nor yours nor mine, so what does it matter? Get dressed.

WILL
(Squirming his way into the clothes) So, Cutting Ball... what's your Christian name?

CUTTING BALL
By the holy piss of John the Baptist, what does Christ have to do with a name? One name's as good as the next, and I've earned Cutting Ball, haven't I?

WILL
Oh?

CUTTING BALL
When I was a lad, I was a bit careless with my knife while lifting purses. *(He mimes slitting one of WILL's testicles)*

WILL
Lovely.

CUTTING BALL
Let's get to work.

(CUTTING BALL and WILL take up positions next to Gifford's door. Crowds pass them, but no one looks carefully at them)

CUTTING BALL
Here we are: Gifford's door.

WILL
Shouldn't we be across the street? He'll see us.

CUTTING BALL
And what if the crowds hide him? No, best be here.

(They watch and wait for a bit. Then a RUFFLER appears, in mean clothes, eyeing them darkly)

CUTTING BALL
(Leaping to his feet and closing with the RUFFLER)
Oi! Clear off, rabbit-sucker! We've got this patch today!

(The RUFFLER gives him the fig, but stalks away)

WILL
You know him?

CUTTING BALL
Aye. A Ruffler.

WILL
Ruffler?

CUTTING BALL
A Ruffler's one who's been to war, and sees

begging as too low an occupation. But he'll beat
you senseless for a groat.

WILL
Are there lots of them?

CUTTING BALL
Enough to have a name.

WILL
And how many types of scoundrels are there
with names?

CUTTING BALL
Well, there's the Coney-Catcher, or confidence
man. That's us today. Your Abram-man pretends
madness. And then—

*(WILL starts suddenly as he sees HELENA passing
down the street)*

WILL
Lady Helena? (He awkwardly tries to hide
himself)

CUTTING BALL
Stop that, you fool. You're drawing eyes.

WILL
It's one of the queen's ladies-in-waiting. She
knows me. Or, she'd recognize me—

CUTTING BALL
Not as a beggar. So show her what she'd expect
to see.

*(WILL relaxes. HELENA passes right by them with
barely a glance, dropping a coin in WILL's palm)*

CUTTING BALL
See? Your coney-catching is just like being a

player on the stage: know your role, know your setting, know your audience, and people will see what you want them to see.

(GIFFORD comes out of his door and stumbles into CUTTING BALL)

GIFFORD
Out of my way, you filth! *(He kicks CUTING BALL and takes off down the street)*

CUTTING BALL
Come on, then.

(They trail GIFFORD through the streets, at a distance)

CUTTING BALL
So you've gotten on Greene's evil side, have you?

WILL
Have I?

CUTTING BALL
He asked me to rough you up.

WILL
It's my own fault. He reminded me of someone.

CUTTING BALL
A lardy rake with loads of brain but no sense?

WILL
(Laughing) Yes, but with less brain.

CUTTING BALL
I know him for what he is. My sis loves him, which makes him family. And he had an open purse, back when he was in funds. Poor luck for him his wife's cut him off.

WILL
Greene's married?

(LUCY appears with an armed SOLDIER. They stop in front of a door. WILL stares in shock)

LUCY
Go on. Get him.

WILL
O! No...

CUTTING BALL
Come on! We're losing Gifford!

(GIFFORD disappears around a corner)

WILL
No, no, no, no, no...

CUTTING BALL
What is it? You know this man?

(The SOLDIER breaks the door and enters the house. LUCY stands outside)

WILL
Aye. And I owe him. Sir Thomas Lucy. Knight, Catholic-hunter, M.P. for Warwickshire, Magistrate of Stratford... and the man who flayed the skin from my back with his own hand.

CUTTING BALL
The devil you say!

WILL
What's Lucy doing in London, on this street, on this day?

(The SOLDIER re-enters, hauling a struggling

DIBDALE, who wears a crucifix and long black robes)

LUCY
Robert Dibdale. I, Sir Thomas Lucy, arrest you in the name of good Queen Elizabeth.

CUTTING BALL
Bold fool. A Papist, hiding a stone's throw of Westminster.

LUCY
Wherever you run, wherever you hide, I will always find you, Catholic scum!

DIBDALE
Neighbors! Now is the time! Overthrow the heretics of England—

(LUCY delivers a cracking blow across DIBDALE's face. DIBDALE collapses, bleeding profusely)

WILL
Bastard!

LUCY
(Hearing WILL's cry, he turns on him) Did you speak, wretch?

WILL
Master!

(WILL bends low, stretches out his hands, and starts crossing to LUCY)

CUTTING BALL
(Aside to WILL) What are you doing?

WILL
(Aside to CUTTING BALL) Showing him what

he expects to see. *(To LUCY)* Alms, master! Pillicock, Pillicock sat on a hill! If he's not gone, he sits there still!

(LUCY steps close and examines WILL. WILL keeps his face averted)

WILL
Alms for Poor Tom?

(WILL clutches at LUCY. LUCY strikes him)

LUCY
No alms for you, fellow! Not when you malign the good name of Thomas! Off with you, vagabond, before I share this Papist's fate with thee!

(WILL scrambles away and CUTTING BALL joins him)

CUTTING BALL
By Saint George's dripping lizard, you're a bold one, I'll give you that.

(WILL and CUTTING BALL exit. LUCY watches them depart with interest. He motions for the SOLDIER to take DIBDALE away, and then he follows after WILL. The scene shifts to the White Hart. WILL and CUTTING BALL enter to find KIT, GREENE, LYLY, and EM drinking and carousing)

WILL
Glad to know while I've been carrying hods in Egypt, you've been toiling so diligently.

KIT
Ah, well, you see, we were all a-nerves for you and attempted to quell our jangling with spirits.

Any luck with Gifford?

CUTTING BALL
We lost him. There was… *(He looks at WILL, who gives him a "not now" look)* some excitement. We'll resume our watch tomorrow. Tonight we drink.

KIT, LYLY, GREENE & EM
Yay!

WILL
I'm going to turn in.

KIT, LYLY, CUTTING BALL & EM
No!

KIT
Join us, Will! These are the times – hale friends, heady wine, and hearty banter – that we're fighting to save. Well, and our lives, of course.

GREENE
A life without wine is a life not worth living.

KIT
Come. Sit. Drink!

WILL
What were you discussing?

KIT, LYLY, GREENE & EM
The lawsuit!

LYLY
Brayne's widow wants the Theatre, but Hyde and the Burbages mean to cut her out.

KIT
Burbage! Pumpkin-nosed mangler of the words of better men!

LYLY
He means to mount Kyd's Spanish Tragedie and make it his own.

GREENE
There is a serious lack in the world, if a play such as that can draw so many ears.

WILL
Someone should write a play about an English king.

GREENE
O! Daring! You'd either be rich, or be hanged.

LYLY
That would depend on the quality of the outcome, no doubt.

GREENE
Or the quality of the king.

LYLY
Which begs the question: who was England's greatest king?

KIT, CUTTING BALL & EM
Henry the Fifth.

GREENE
What? Because he died before he could grow old?

EM
He won the battle of Azincourt!

GREENE
A battle, a marriage, an heir, then death – that's his whole legacy.

LYLY
Well, what are kings are famous for? Henry the
Fifth for a battle.

GREENE
Henry the Eighth for marital folly and material
fatness. *(He pats his own belly)*

WILL
No, for religion.

(A chorus of "Ayes" passes through the group)

LYLY
Let's look further back. Richard the Lionheart?

KIT
Or his father, who married the French girl and
nearly conquered the world.

GREENE
If you admire conquerors, what of Edward
Longshanks?

KIT
I prefer his son, most memorable for his end.

CUTTING BALL
For a blazing hot poker up his end, you mean.

LYLY
What of his son? Edward the Third ruled for
decades, and had more than one victory.

KIT
He began the Hundred Years War. It took Henry
the Fifth to end it.

WILL
Personally, I would argue that our greatest king
is our queen.

ALL
Long may she reign.

GREENE
But she has failed in her one duty – to provide
us with an heir.

LYLY
Which begs another question – what's the best
gift a monarch can leave to posterity? A great
victory, lasting peace, or an heir?

KIT
Victory.

CUTTING BALL & EM
Victory.

GREENE
An heir.

LYLY
I say peace. Will?

WILL
(Struck with inspiration) An idea. (As the room
falls still) How many people have left something
new behind them? How many have changed the
world with their very being? Too few. Hector.
Moses. The first Brutus.

LYLY
Aristotle. Socrates.

KIT
Caesar.

LYLY
Christ.

GREENE
Mohammad.

KIT
Constantine.

LYLY
Chaucer.

CUTTING BALL
King Arthur.

EM
Martin Luther.

GREENE
Dante.

KIT
Machiavelli.

WILL
Yes! I submit the greatest legacy we can leave behind is a new idea.

KIT
And what idea do you mean to leave behind?

WILL
How can I answer? I haven't thought of it. Yet.

(Late the next day, WILL and CUTTING BALL are at their post across from Gifford's door. It's gray, drizzling dewy rain. GIFFORD finally emerges from his house and takes off into the city, moving more furtively than before. WILL and CUTTING BALL follow)

CUTTING BALL
Gifford's leaving later today, eh? And see how he's walking? More careful-like? This may be it.

(GIFFORD ducks into an alley, where he meets with a cloaked figure)

CUTTING BALL
And who's this, now?

(The figure turns his head, revealing his face. It is SAVAGE)

WILL
Oh-ho.

CUTTING BALL
Know him?

WILL
His name's Savage. Catholic agent. Looks like he survived the bear. What do we do now?

CUTTING BALL
Follow him, find where he lives, and search his rooms. Does he know you?

WILL
Yes.

CUTTING BALL
Then you're out. I'll follow him myself.

WILL
And then?

CUTTING BALL
I'll do what needs to be done.

WILL
You'd risk yourself like that?

CUTTING BALL
She's my queen, too, isn't she? Go on, get yourself back to the White Hart.

(GIFFORD exits one way. SAVAGE exits another and CUTTING BALL follows him. WILL remains for a moment, profoundly struck by CUTTING BALL's patriotic sentiment)

WILL

(Aside) She's his queen too. O! Cutting Ball, the Wits, Emily – all of them – there's more life in these low beings, these clowns and vagabonds, than all the highborn lords of the court. Yes, someone should write plays about our kings, but these creatures are no less worthy of immortality. *(He walks through the city, letting the rain fall freely over him)* And look at this place! For all its filth and danger... washed clean by rainfall, London is the perfect place to re-create one's self. The scholars say there's nothing new, that everything in creation was already made by the Creator. But reality is not perception, and the perception of newness can make a thing seem new again. And if perception can make something new to a person, might not a person make himself new to perception? *(Feeling a sense of freedom he's not felt in a long time, he removes his ragged beggar's shirt and wipes his face clean)* My destiny is not fixed. I needn't be Will False-staff forever. I can be William—

LUCY

SHAKESPEARE!!!

(As WILL reaches the White Hart, he is surprised by LUCY and two of his SOLIDERS lying in ambush. WILL cringes and looks for a quick exit, but LUCY and his SOLIDIERS move to block his way)

LUCY
I wager you haven't heard that name in some time, have you? I've been asking around. Sounds like you go by Falstaff now? "Shake-spear" becomes "False-staff" – a weak jest to hide your true surname. O! How I've longed for this day.

WILL
How did you find me?

LUCY
I merely followed a certain suspicious lunatic. I wasn't sure at first. But the look in those eyes... I knew it from somewhere. That pride. Now come along, and try to die like a man.

WILL
I'm not armed.

LUCY
And if you were, would it make any difference? You never knew foible from pommel.

WILL
I know your foibles for what they are, Sir Thomas Lousy.

LUCY
(*Drawing his blade*) There it is again! That damned Shakespearean pride! I thought I lashed it out of you. But then you killed poor Johnson.

LUCY SOLDIER 1
Murderer!

LUCY
Seems you need another lesson.

WILL
You'd beat an unarmed man in the street? Of

course you would. That's your specialty–

LUCY
Be warned! There is a fair price on your head,
Master Shakestaff. I could stab you now and–

WILL
Your favored means of gaining gold – the murder
of innocent men.

LUCY
Innocent!?Your family plotted with the Catholics!
And do you deny breaking Johnson's pate and
leaving him to die, Shakestaff? Or should I call
you Quiverstaff, given how you tremble at my
approach?

WILL
Call me what you please. I've already named you,
Sir Too Mouse-y Louse-y.

LUCY
(Twitching) Don't you dare–

WILL
A parliament member, a justice of peace,
At home a poore scarecrow, in London an asse,
If Lucy be Lowsie as some folke misscall it
Then Lowsie is Lucy whatever befall it.

LUCY
Silence!

(LUCY stabs at WILL's chest. WILL twists sideways
and raises his arm. The point of the blade passes
just below his armpit. WILL clamps his arm down,
locking the blade, and strikes the wrist of LUCY's
sword arm. The sword comes free and WILL reverses
it, pointing the blade under LUCY's chin)

WILL
He thinks himself greate, yet an asse in his state
We allow by his eares but with asses to mate;
If Lucy be Lowsie as some folk misscall it,
Then Lowsie is Lucy whatever befall it.

*(LUCY ducks backward and away from the blade,
seeking safety behind his SOLDIERS)*

LUCY
Get him, you fools!

*(The SOLDIERS attack WILL. WILL's desperation
grows as he must parry attacks from both sides)*

WILL
To the sessions he went and did sorely complain
His parke had been rob'd, and his deer they were slain.
If Lucy be Lowsie as some folk misscall it,
Then Lowsie is Lucy whatever befall it.

LUCY
Stop his mouth!

WILL
Kit Marlowe, where are you!?

*(Things look grim for WILL. Then, with a great cry,
KIT bounds out of a second story window of the
White Hart, landing on one of the SOLDIERS and
sending him sprawling)*

KIT
Well, well! Who needs rescuing now?

*(LUCY takes up the fallen SOLDIER's sword and
the fight continues)*

WILL
So haughty was he when the fact was confess'd

He sayd 'twas a crime that could not be redress'd.
Though Lucies a dozen he paints in his coat
His name it shall Lousy for Lucy be wrote.

(KIT dispatches the second SOLDIER. WILL bests LUCY and places his sword to the knight's chest)

WILL
If a juvenille frolick he cannot forgive
We'll sing Lowsie Lucy as long as we live!

(WILL leans in close to LUCY)

WILL
By the way - your deer was delicious.

(WILL knocks LUCY to the ground in a humiliating fashion, then WILL and KIT flee)

LUCY
Shakespeare, you murderer! I'll be revenged!

(Escaping, WILL and KIT step aside into a narrow alley)

KIT
So. Shakespeare. Is that your real name?

WILL
Aye. *(He starts to laugh)*

KIT
Why on earth are you laughing?

WILL
I've imagined encountering him again so many times, always fearing it would be the end of my story. Instead, I've lived to fight another day!

KIT
"If Lucy be Lowsie as some folk misscall it, then

Lowsie is Lucy whatever befall it." What does that even mean?

WILL
Who knows? When Lucy was done whipping me, I wanted to call him a louse in as many ways as I could, so I devised that little poetic revenge. Poor stuff, but he vowed vengeance.

KIT
Lucy called you murderer. Who was the victim?

WILL
Johnson. One of Lucy's men. *(Deciding how to tell the story)* I was carting my drunken father home late one night and we met Johnson on the road. He tried to take me in for another flogging. My father said... some things he shouldn't have. There was a fight. Soon, Johnson was lying on his face, his head broken, with a log beside him covered in blood. So I kissed my wife and children farewell, and fled before Lucy had me hanged.

KIT
Wait. Wife!?

WILL
Aye. Anne. Another tale for another time.

KIT
Well, now: after all that, please tell me you discovered something today.

WILL
Gifford met with our dear friend Savage, and then Cutting Ball followed him to ground. But how will we find him now that we can't go back to the White Hart?

KIT
I know where Cutting Ball keeps his lair. Come.

(KIT leads WILL to a ramshackle residence. KIT knocks and EM opens the door a crack)

KIT
Is your brother about?

EM
He's not with you?

KIT
Fut. We need a place to hide.

EM
Come on. The boys just got here.

(EM leads them to an interior room, where they find GREENE and LYLY)

GREENE
It's mayhem at the White Hart, Christopher. What did you do?

KIT
Me?! For once, this wasn't my fault.

(CUTTING BALL enters, climbing through a window)

CUTTING BALL
Somehow, I find that hard to believe.

WILL
Cutting Ball!

CUTTING BALL
Look what I've got. (He produces a small piece of paper with four short lines of text on it)

WILL
The code! *(He takes it and starts writing out the decoded message)*

KIT
You were able to follow Savage?

CUTTING BALL
Aye. He's staying in a Deptford inn. I waited till he left, then let myself in.

LYLY
You stole the code key from his room? He'll know it's missing!

CUTTING BALL
I'm no fool. I made a copy.

LYLY
You can read?

CUTTING BALL
Anyone with half a brain can copy letters.

WILL
(Finishing the decoding) There.

(They look at it, perplexed)

KIT
What?

GREENE
"Erap erpy ade?"

EM
What language is that?

WILL
(In a fury) Another code! A code within the code! We're no further along than before.

LYLY
But, wait. O, clever for its very simplicity! Tis
a mirror! You see? They just wrote the message
backwards before encoding it. *(He reads the
message in reverse)* "Elizabeth dies at Theatre
August Third. The heavens shall raine down
upon Elizabeth. Fire and Hell will swallow only
noble soules. Rescue Mary same day. Prepare."

WILL
August Third? But that's...

KIT
Tomorrow. Damn, damn, and damn.

GREENE
"The heavens shall raine down..." They waste a
lot of coded space on hyperbole.

WILL
What do we do? Is this the information that
saves us? If we take it to Walsingham—

KIT
He'll put us to death and save the Queen himself.

WILL
But surely we're not the priority here! This is
the Queen's life at stake.

KIT
Yes, and the Queen's men mean to have us dead.
There is delicious irony in rescuing Her Majesty
under the noses of the very men who are busy
protecting her from us.

WILL
Kit... Christopher. We cannot play at this.

KIT

On the contrary, the play's the thing! We must
find what play she's attending, and where. Usually
the players go to her, but once in a great while
she attends the theatre in secret.

LYLY

Well, that's easy enough. The only public play on
Sunday is at the Newington Butts. The Spanish
Tragedie got special exemption to perform on
the holy day of rest.

KIT

Of course, because the Queen will be present,
but they're not making that part public. So, we
know she'll be there. And that she'll be attacked.
What do we do?

WILL

I've got it. We pose as players.

GREENE
(In unison) What!?

LYLY
(In unison) No!!

CUTTING BALL
(In unison) Are you a fool?

EM
(In unison) Will—

KIT

O! Brilliant! We'll have the run of the theatre
without question, so we can foil whatever scheme
they have.

LYLY

Pistols, for certain. 'Raine fire?' They mean to

use pistols to fire up from the crowd and bring
Her Majesty low.

KIT
And from the stage we can see the whole crowd,
pick out where the villains stand, and disrupt
them when they try.

GREENE
And how, pray, do you achieve this end? You
can't very well walk up to the Earl of Oxford's
Men and demand parts.

KIT
(Inspiration strikes) That's where you come in.

GREENE
Me!?

KIT
We'll need to pretend to be players fresh from...
say, Cambridge, and given entrance to the London
theatrical scene by that most pre-eminent man
of letters, Monsieur Greene.

GREENE
But the rolls are set! How can I—

KIT
(Eyes twinkling) It's a part only you can play. Find
two members of Oxford's company and drink
them senseless. Put that girth of yours to good
use and dare them to match you, cup for cup.
Afterwards, when they lie as in a death, offer us
up as their replacements!

GREENE
Very well. *(Tragi-heroically)* If I am called upon
to bravely indulge in the fruit of the vine to

save Her Majesty, then this is the sacrifice I must make. Em, don't wait up. Come on, Lyly – let's go destroy some actors.

(GREENE and LYLY exit)

CUTTING BALL
Someone better watch their backs.

EM
Keep 'em safe, Bally-boy.

(Nodding, CUTTING BALL exits)

KIT
We should rest. We have a trying day ahead of us.

WILL
Go on. I won't be long.

(KIT gives WILL a sideways look, but exits to an interior room. EM starts to exit)

WILL
Emily, wait. *(He starts to speak but hesitates)*

EM
Something on your mind?

WILL
I need... I need you to carry a message for me.

EM
Why me?

WILL
You're the only one that can get close enough without raising suspicion. It may be dangerous.

EM
Will it help protect the Queen?

WILL
I hope it will.

EM
Then damn your dangers and doubts. Tell me.

(Late that night, LYLY enters Cutting Ball's leveraging the bulk of an impossibly intoxicated GREENE)

GREENE
(Singing) AND THE RAIN IT RAINETH EVR'Y DAY...

KIT
Greene? Good God, man, you look terrible.

GREENE
You don't know me...

LYLY
I've never seen anything like it. Songs will be sung about this night.

GREENE
I drink for my queen... she's a special lady...

LYLY
He's down for now, but he played his part and kept his word. *(He hands over two rolls of paper)* These are your rolls.

KIT
I never doubted him. Just make sure he's recovered for tomorrow.

(LYLY exits with GREENE)

WILL
Who are you playing?

KIT
(Examining his roll) Villuppo. Which was he?

WILL
The man who falsely accuses Alexandro in the opening scene. *(Checking his roll)* And I'm Alexandro.

KIT
Ha! Perfect. And I am to die, am I not? Excellent! We'll con these in the morning.

WILL
When do we rehearse with the rest?

KIT
(Scoffing) Plays don't rehearse! The prompter will direct you to enter here, exit there, dance at this bit, and we're off!

WILL
What have I done? This is a ridiculous plan.

KIT
It's sublime! They'll be watching the crowd for trouble-makers, but whose eyes will be on the stage?

WILL
Everyone's!

KIT
Precisely! And they will see two magnificently handsome young men in false beards and Portuguese attire, speaking poor lines so splendidly that they'll never doubt we're the finest actors of the age! The Queen herself will weep my death!

WILL
This is a terrible plan.

KIT
We'll find out for certain tomorrow. Tomorrow,
tomorrow, tomorrow...

*(The next day, WILL and KIT report backstage at
the Newington Butts Theatre)*

KIT
Let's find the Prompter.

EVANS
(Approaching) Who the devil are you?

WILL
Ah... They said to report to you.

EVANS
And you are?

WILL
Will... Lancet. And, er...

KIT
(Putting on a voice) Christopher Sly.

WILL
The replacement players.

EVANS
About damned time. Conned the text, I hope?

WILL
Aye.

EVANS
Good. You enter at the third trumpet. *(Calling
offstage)* Augie! Augustine!

(AUGUSTINE enters)

AUGUSTINE
What ho, Hank?

EVANS

These are your Alexandro and Villuppo for today. Take charge of them, will you? I have enough to trouble me with the new stagehands. *(He exits)*

WILL

(To AUGUSTINE, rather star-struck) You're the Viceroy! I saw the play the other day and you were simply wonderful—

AUGUSTINE

Fine, fine. All right, so you enter with me from the lower stage right door. *(As WILL starts to head in the wrong direction)* No, no, stage right! Fools think because they can talk they can act...

(He leads them to their place as EVANS re-enters with costumes for WILL and KIT)

EVANS: Costumes. *(He exits)*

AUGUSTINE

After our first bit, that's the end of us till Act Two, though you two play ladies in the background – there are wigs and dresses for you. Just follow the others and stay close to the stage wall. Don't know why I'm the one has to tell you all this. Bloody Hank. Anyway, I'll fetch you for our entrances.

(WILL and KIT prepare for the performance, applying their false beards and dressing in fine robes)

AUGUSTINE

And, if I may offer a word of well-intended advice – too many men ascending the stage feel the need to gesticulate, slash the air with their hands, or slap their thighs. Speak loudly and clearly, but keep your hands still, so that when you do make use of them, it is to greater effect. And remember, though your character addresses me, you must address the crowd. I know what you are to say, they do not. That's all, I think. If you lose your line, press on, and I'll assist as best I can. The rest, as they say, is a mystery.

(Trumpets sound. AUGUSTINE takes up position near the stage right door. WILL and KIT follow)

KIT
Ah, William! The trumpets blare, sounding our imminent victory over our woes, our foes, and our sorrows!

WILL
Stop talking.

(Trumpets sound again)

KIT
What happens before us, again?

WILL
Revenge and Don Andrea. Then–

(Trumpets sound again)

AUGUSTINE
Go!

(AUGUSTINE pushes WILL and KIT onstage and follows)

AUGUSTINE (AS THE VICEROY)
Is our embassador dispatcht for Spaine?

(WILL takes in the scene, takes a breath, and speaks)

WILL (AS ALEXANDRO)
Two days, my liege, are past since his depart.

AUGUSTINE (AS THE VICEROY)
And tribute payment gone along with him?

WILL (AS ALEXANDRO)
Aye, my good Lord.

*(AUGUSTINE delivers a long speech downstage –
falling dramatically to the ground after a few lines –
as WILL and KIT scan the crowd and surreptitiously
talk to each other behind him)*

KIT
Is the Queen here? Do you see her?

WILL
Up there.

*(WILL nods in the direction of a PAINTED
WOMAN in the top box, muffled in a voluminous
cloak. CUTTING BALL, GREENE, and LYLY
become visible among the groundlings)*

KIT
Good. And there's Cutting Ball. And Greene and
Lyly. Our band of brothers.

WILL
All right. Now we just need to find Savage.
*(Suddenly spying LUCY in one of the boxes, he
freezes)* O! No...

*(As WILL and KIT stare in shock at LUCY,
AUGUSTINE finishes his speech)*

AUGUSTINE (AS THE VICEROY)
My death were naturall! But his was forced!

*(AUGUSTINE glares at WILL as WILL stares at
LUCY)*

AUGUSTINE (AS THE VICEROY)
My death were naturall! But his was forced!
His was—

(KIT kicks WILL)

WILL (AS ALEXANDRO)
O wicked forgery! O traitorous miscreant!

EVANS
(Poking his head onstage, stage whispering) The
proper line is, "No doubt, my liege—"

KIT
(Aside, to EVANS) Thanks, Hank! *(Ignoring
EVANS' prompt, KIT steps forward picks up a previ-
ous section of the scene)*

KIT (AS VILLUPPO)
But, no! Hear the truth—

EVANS
(From the side of the stage) No.

KIT (AS VILLUPPO)
Which these mine eyes—

EVANS
(From the side of the stage) No!!

KIT (AS VILLUPPO)
Have seen—

AUGUSTINE (AS THE VICEROY)
Hold thy peace—

KIT (AS VILLUPPO)
But my sovereign—

AUGUSTINE (AS THE VICEROY)
Away with him! His sight is second hell!

Keep him till we determine his death.

(KIT hauls WILL backstage and AUGUSTINE follows, stalking away)

AUGUSTINE
Amateurs...

(WILL and KIT change costumes, donning dresses and wigs)

KIT
What was that?

WILL
Thomas Lucy is here!

KIT
I know, but you skipped all my lines! How am I supposed to dazzle the Queen?

WILL
What does this mean? Is he just taking in the play? Or have we been betrayed?

KIT
Our task is the same. Only now we must achieve it before Lucy recognizes you.

(They are joined by THE ACTOR PLAYING BEL-IMPERIA as the bustle of backstage life passes all around them. WILL spots a STAGEHAND hauling a small barrel towards the cannons. He speaks quietly to KIT, making sure THE ACTOR PLAYING BEL-IMPERIA doesn't hear)

WILL
Kit. Look.

KIT
What, the stagehand? What about him?

WILL
He's got a barrel of powder!

KIT
Of course. I'm sure he mans the cannons at the end of the play.

WILL
Kit. The cannons.

KIT
O! Turn them, fill them with shot, and poof, no Queen. "Fire and Hell" indeed. *(Crossing to the STAGEHAND)* Say, aren't the cannons dangerous?

STAGEHAND
Hardly! There's no shot, just powder. *(He pats the barrel)*

ACTOR PLAYING BEL-IMPERIA
And I thought I was the ball-less one today.

STAGEHAND
(Ignoring the actor) Besides, we're not firing – some noble out there paid extra. Afraid of the noise. Probably for the best, with the usual crew gone.

KIT
Where'd they go?

STAGEHAND
Some fancy French ship hired an army of hands this morning. I heard too late, or I'd've gone myself!

WILL
So who are the other hands I've seen around?

STAGEHAND
No idea. Replacements, I guess.

ACTOR PLAYING BEL-IMPERIA
Ladies! We're on!

(WILL and KIT follow the ACTOR PLAYING BEL-IMPERIA onstage, where he meets the ACTOR PLAYING HORATIO. WILL and KIT cling to the rear wall)

ACTOR PLAYING HORATIO
Now, madam, since by favor of your love
Our hidden smoke is turned to open flame...

(The scene continues as WILL and KIT surreptitiously talk to each other upstage)

KIT
All right, so they arranged for the stagehands to find better employment, and, like us, have taken the place of the missing men.

WILL
They're going to fire the cannon into the crowd at the end of the show.

KIT
Then our answer is simple – we douse the powder. Wet, it shall not ignite. Leave it to me.

(The scene ends, and they cross backstage again. As WILL resumes his previous costume, KIT crosses to the STAGEHAND)

KIT
I need a scroll for the next scene. Do you know where I could find one?

STAGEHAND
Aye. I'll get one for you. (Exits)

(KIT grabs a water skin from a nearby table and empties it in the barrel of powder. The STAGEHAND returns and hands KIT a scroll)

KIT
Thanks, friend. *(He returns to WILL and quickly re-dresses in his first costume)* There! That's put paid to our Savage friend.

WILL
I hope so.

KIT
When's our next scene?

WILL
The way this play is flying by, it can't be long–

(AUGUSTINE enters with the ACTOR PLAYING THE NOBLE-MAN. AUGUSTINE hands WILL a pair of shackles)

AUGUSTINE
Our scene is next. Here, you need to wear these manacles. Now, keep your wits about you this time, eh? *(To KIT)* Come on, you. *(He exits onstage with KIT)*

THE ACTOR PLAYING THE NOBLE-MAN
(Helping WILL into the manacles) Let me help you with those.

WILL
O! Do they have to be so tight?

THE ACTOR PLAYING THE NOBLE-MAN
(Ignoring WILL's complaint) I've got the key, so

make sure you find me after the scene.

WILL
These things are real? Umm...

THE ACTOR PLAYING THE NOBLE-MAN
Go!

(The ACTOR PLAYING THE NOBLE-MAN pushes WILL onstage)

AUGUSTINE (AS THE VICEROY)
Why linger ye? Bring forth that daring feend,
And let him die for his accursed deed.

(WILL is bound to one of the pillars. Then he sees SAVAGE across the way, passing through the back-stage area carrying a small covered lamp)

WILL
(Aside) There he is! John Savage. With fire. O!
What do I do? Cry out? It might only warn him,
give him the time he needs to take action. And
who knows how many confederates he has here.
Do I play out the scene? What am I doing?

AUGUSTINE (AS THE VICEROY)
To the tortures! Burn his body in those flames!

(WILL is menaced with torches as lights rise on the PAINTED WOMAN in her box)

WILL
(Aside) To act, despite the risk – or not to act.
That's the question. My country may not love me,
but I love my country. And my Queen. And she
must live. (Thoughts coming to him faster than
they can tumble out) For what have I to lose?
My life? What is life? A tale told by an idiot, full
of... what? Piss and vinegar? Something! But it

never ran smoothly. So what am I waiting for? Cowards die many times before their deaths; the brave only once. Yes! Don't be afraid of greatness. I know what I am, but not what I may be. It's not the stars' fault, but our own, if we fail. Whoa. What's happening? *(Collecting himself:)* I'm going to save her. Do you hear me, O Heavens? I'm going to— *(Casting his gaze up to the painted Heavens, high above the stage floor, he suddenly gets it)* Heavens... O!

(WILL breaks free from the pillar as the actors onstage acknowledge that he shouldn't have done so yet)

KIT
(To the other ACTORS) I've got this.

(KIT takes the stage and, determined to get his big speech out, jumps ahead in the scene)

KIT (AS VILLUPPO)
(Over-dramatically)
O! Rent with remembrance of so foule a deed...

WILL
(Aside to KIT) Kit!

KIT (AS VILLUPPO)
My guiltie soule submits me to thy doome...

WILL
(Aside to KIT) Now's not the time!

KIT (AS VILLUPPO)
(Slowing down to extend his moment in the spotlight)
For, not for Alexandros injuries...

(WILL knees KIT in the gut, causing him to double over)

WILL (AS ALEXANDRO)
(To AUGUSTINE) What says my lord? Shall I take the villain hence? I'll take him hence! Fie! I am thus resolved!

(WILL hauls KIT offstage. The ACTOR PLAYING THE NOBLE-MAN removes the shackle from WILL's right arm, but — in a desperate hurry — WILL brushes him away before he can remove the other)

WILL
Leave it. I'll get it later. Kit! *(He pulls KIT aside)*

KIT
What was that? Was I too good? Is that it? I didn't know you were the jealous sort.

WILL
Kit! The Heavens!

KIT
What are you—

WILL
What did you say they called the roof above the stage?

KIT
Yes, they're called the Heavens, for heaven's sake. Now why—

WILL
"The Heavens shall raine down upon Elizabeth!" I saw Savage with a lantern just before I came onstage.

KIT
O! What blind beetles we are! Come, Will! Pray we're not too late.

(WILL grabs his sword and he and KIT race up the ladder to the Heavens. It is a low-ceilinged space, light coming in through chinks and slats in the thatched roof. In the center of the floor is a rope-drawn wheel hanging above a trap door – the deus ex machina. The space is filled with barrels, all marked with a chalked fish. WILL reaches in one and pulls out a handful of black gunpowder)

WILL
O! Dear Lord.

KIT
There's enough gunpowder here to blow the theatre to pieces.

(Hearing sounds from below, WILL and KIT hide. SAVAGE and ROOKWOOD enter the Heavens; both are armed. SAVAGE has the lantern; it is lit but the doors are currently shut. ROOKWOOD carries a small barrel and pours out a trail of gunpowder leading to the explosive cache)

ROOKWOOD
When do we light it?

SAVAGE
We need to time it for the end of the play – no doubt Elizabeth will come to the stage itself. We'll light the powder trail with just enough time to get ourselves out of here.

KIT
(Aside to WILL) What do we do?

(Thinking to act, WILL rises. The loose manacle on WILL's hand accidentally strikes the side of a barrel)

SAVAGE
Who's there?!

WILL
Kit! Quick! Quench that flame!

(A tense battle ensues. WILL and KIT try to scatter the powder trail and wrest the lantern from SAVAGE as the four combatants fight in incredibly tight quarters. Soon, SAVAGE gets the lantern doors open)

ROOKWOOD
Wait! Savage! Not while we're up here!

SAVAGE
I'm willing to die if I must. Are not you?

ROOKWOOD
Fut that!

(SAVAGE makes to hurl the lantern onto the powder trail, but WILL throws himself on it and holds tight. There is a violent struggle, one which SAVAGE looks to surely win. In desperation, WILL takes the open end of his manacle, slams it on SAVAGE's wrist. Looking down, he notices that he's standing atop the trap door)

WILL
(To himself) Deus ex machina! *(Yelling to KIT)* Kit! Throw the lever!

KIT
Are you sure?

WILL
Do it!

(KIT throws the lever and the trap door opens beneath WILL and SAVAGE. They tumble through space,

manacled together, towards the stage floor below)

WILL & SAVAGE
Aaaaaaaaaaaa!!!!!!!!!

(SAVAGE lands first, hard. WILL lands atop him, slightly cushioning his fall. They land in front of AUGUSTINE, startling him mightily)

AUGUSTINE
Great Caesar's ghost!

(AUGUSTINE flees the stage as SAVAGE spies the PAINTED WOMAN in her box and roars to his feet)

SAVAGE
Sic semper tyrannis!

(The Newington Butts erupts in chaos. From among the groundlings, GREENE and LYLY appear)

LYLY
Protect the Queen!

GREENE
(To SAVAGE) Back, you varlet!

LYLY
(To SAVAGE) You'll not touch a hair on Her Majesty's head!

(SAVAGE moves towards the PAINTED WOMAN, dragging WILL behind him. GREENE, LYLY, and CUTTING BALL intercede. They all battle SAVAGE, but SAVAGE fights with monstrous strength)

SAVAGE
Let me at her! Death to the Queen!

(CUTTING BALL emerges from the crowd and joins the melee)

CUTTING BALL
Save a piece for me!

(CUTTING BALL, GREENE, LYLY, and WILL all pile on SAVAGE. Impossibly, SAVAGE fights on. Just as it seems the man will never drop, KIT slides down the rope from the Heavens and lands on SAVAGE, finally driving him down)

KIT
Well, that was easy enough. *(Preening proudly for the PAINTED WOMAN, he presses his blade to SAVAGE's neck)* And now this villain will pay—

WILL, LYLY, GREENE & CUTTING BALL
No!

WILL
Keep him alive! He must stand trial!

KIT
(Greatly disappointed) Very well... *(He clubs SAVAGE with the pommel of his sword, knocking him unconscious)*

WILL
Where's the key to these damned shackles?

CUTTING BALL
Allow me. *(He expertly undoes the shackles)*

LUCY
(Approaching, sword drawn) Stay where you are! William Shakespeare, I arrest you in the Queen's name!

LYLY
Are you mad?!

GREENE
Who do you think you are?

LUCY
Sir Thomas Lucy, magistrate and Member of
Parliament. And you will all be hanged!

PAINTED WOMAN
Silence, all of you!

*(All heads turn and then all knees bow as the
PAINTED WOMAN makes her way to the stage)*

ALL
Your Majesty!

PAINTED WOMAN
(To LUCY) You say they will be hanged? What is
the charge?

LUCY
(Perplexed) Why... the attempted assassination of
Her Majesty the Queen.

PAINTED WOMAN
How can that be? When the Queen is not even
present?

*(The PAINTED WOMAN throws back her cowl,
revealing herself as HELENA. All stare in amaze-
ment)*

KIT
Lady Helena! How did you— *(Turning on WILL in
outrage)* O! You told her!

WILL
I may have...

KIT
How could you? It was our one chance to impress the Queen!

WILL
I could not, in conscience, allow Her Majesty's life to be risked. Though when I sent you my message, Lady Helena, I didn't mean for you to take her place. You risked too much.

HELENA
No more than you, Master Falstaff. Or is it Shakespeare now?

LUCY
(To HELENA) I don't know who you are, but William Shakespeare is a murderer, and I'm taking him back to Stratford to be flogged and hanged!

HELENA
I know not who you are, sir, but I'm certain this man is innocent.

WILL
I'm afraid I am so charged, my lady. He has the right to take me.

HELENA
I think that you do not belong to this man, or any other. I think you are a woman's man.

KIT
Ummm—

HELENA
And that woman is the Queen. Ah, see - here is her representative now.

(WALSINGHAM enters)

WALSINGHAM
(Taking in each one in turn) You all have much to answer for.

KIT
(Gaily) Before we press on, could we step outside? There are numerous barrels of gunpowder over our heads, and all this heated talk may explode more than tempers.

WALSINGHAM
(To LUCY) You, stand down. *(To WILL and KIT)* You and you, with me.

LUCY
It'll be the noose for you, Shakespeare!

(WILL bites his thumb at LUCY. He and KIT exit, and the scene shifts to WILL and KIT standing before WALSINGHAM in the spymaster's study)

WALSINGHAM
So. What shall I do with the two of you?

KIT
I know what you should do, Sir Francis.

WALSINGHAM
Fall to my knees and thank God you were here to save the realm? Heap you with praise, honors, and gold? Whisper in Her Majesty's ear about a knighthood?

KIT
Well, if you insist...

WALSINGHAM
Your meddling nearly undermined a year's worth

of careful labor!

KIT
We captured Savage!

WALSINGHAM
I needed him free so to identify his conspirators!

KIT
We saved the Queen!

WALSINGHAM
The Queen wasn't there.

KIT
But she would have been!

WALSINGHAM
(Begrudgingly) I'll grant you that. But while everyone else was following orders, you interfered with my operations. You assaulted agents of the crown. And you've abetted this man, William Shakespeare, a man who, if I am to believe Sir Thomas Lucy, was born a Catholic and is guilty of murder. *(To WILL)* Is there anything in this you wish to contest?

WILL
(After considering for a moment) No, sir.

WALSINGHAM
Fortunate for you, then, it's clear to me that Lucy is an idiot. You didn't kill his man Johnson. You were covering for your father, who I'm told is a drunkard.

WILL
How did you—

WALSINGHAM
Ah, then I'm correct? Gratifying.

KIT
(To WILL) You lied to me?

WALSINGHAM
What was the cause?

WILL
Wine. And pride.

WALSINGHAM
So rather than have your sire branded a murderer,
you fled, letting suspicion fall upon you, thus
sparing his life. Which makes you more of a fool
than Marlowe here.

KIT
Sir Francis, please end this tortuous catting-and-
mousing and tell us what you intend to do with
us.

WALSINGHAM
*(Picking up a handbill for The Spanish Tragedie from
his desk)* Tell me, do you plan to continue a life
in the theatre?

(WILL and KIT exchange surprised glances)

KIT
Is there a correct answer?

WALSINGHAM
It is my hope that you'll answer with an affirma-
tion. Both of you.

KIT
It was my understanding that you detested the
theatre.

WALSINGHAM
No, I detest theatre people. But I respect the
theatre. There are few better tools to alter the
mood of the people – or shape their opinions.
It is my desire that you both remain in London,
and in the arts. In return, I shall... arrange
matters. There will be no knighthood, no gold
or honors. But there will be your lives, for as
long as I see fit to prolong them. Mr. Marlowe,
I will require information from you, and the
occasional service. Master Shakespeare, I have
informed Lucy that as long as you're here,
you're under my eye. But should you venture
outside the city, you will be hanged. There's no
question of returning to Stratford, I'm afraid.
You now belong to Her Majesty the Queen.
Body and soul.

KIT
Her Majesty's Will.

*(The scene shifts to a tavern, where WILL and KIT
join LYLY, GREENE, CUTTING BALL, and
TARLTON. The CHORUS enters aside)*

CHORUS
And so we return to the Elephant – where
Sebastian missed Antonio – one last time. Or is
it the White Hart, where Jack Cade made brave
speeches? The Boar's Head? Or the Centaur?
Take your pick, gentles – they're all the same,
really – and imagine the scene. There would be
cheers.

ALL
(Raising their glasses) Huzzah!

(They embrace, and then TARLTON plays music for the group as KIT takes WILL aside)

CHORUS
Soon there would be music, which is how all Comedies should end, along with a touch of sorrow, everyone wiser than before. And a marriage! Always a marriage! But who was wed that night? Not man and wife, but man and idea.

KIT
Well, all turned out right, did it not? It was a trifle more convoluted than I anticipated—

WILL
A trifle!?

KIT
But all's well that ends well, eh? So, what will it be for you? Will you be an actor?

WILL
The profession has long fascinated me. But... you know, when you first introduced me to the Wits and you University men heaped coals on the head of Thomas Kyd... I thought about writing. About being a playwright.

KIT
Truly?

WILL
Yes. Before then, it would never have occurred to me. How presumptuous, to try to join the ranks of Aristophanes, Terrence, and Ovid! What tanner's son could rise to such heights? But listening to the abuses you all hurled at a humble man of no formal education merely because he dared to reach above himself, to give his thoughts

wings... Then, today, when I stood on that stage, faced with my own mortality, something broke free in me. And it came to me in a flash: I knew what I would do. I will spite all the pompous men of high learning and low morals that would keep me down. I will unearth the world of words that lives within me. I will write plays.

(WILL looks to the CHORUS, who bows to him and exits)

KIT
(After an admiring pause) You know what? Me, too.

WILL
Oh, really?

KIT
Yes. And mine will be so much better.

WILL
A challenge, by my life! Very well. Let the worthiest Wit win.

(WILL kisses KIT to the cheers of all. Lights out)

END OF PLAY

ABOUT THE AUTHOR

Consistently described as 'intricate,' 'taut,' and 'breathtaking', David Blixt's work combines a love of theatre with a deep respect for the quirks and passions
of history. His novels span the early Roman Empire
(the COLOSSUS series, his play EVE OF IDES) to
early Renaissance Italy (the STAR-CROSS'D series)
through the Elizabethan era with HER MAJESTY'S
WILL to 19th Century America with his next novel.

David continues to write, act, and travel. He has ridden
camels around the pyramids at Giza, been thrown out
of the Vatican Museum and been blessed by Pope John-
Paul II, scaled the Roman ramp at Masada, crashed a
hot-air balloon, leapt from cliffs on small Greek is-
lands, dined with Counts and criminals, climbed to
the top of Mount Sinai, and sat in the Prince's chair
in Verona's palace. But David is happiest at his desk,
weaving tales of brilliant people in dire and dramatic
straits. Living in Chicago with his wife and two children, David describes himself as "actor, author, father,
husband. In reverse order."

WWW.DAVIDBLIXT.COM

ABOUT THE PLAYWRIGHT

Robert Kauzlaric has written more than a dozen theatrical adaptations which have been performed in nearly forty states across the U.S., as well as in Ireland, England, and Canada.

The New York Times called his adaptation of THE TRUE STORY OF THE 3 LITTLE PIGS! "One of the best children's shows of the year." His version of H.G. Wells' THE ISLAND OF DR. MOREAU received five of Chicago's Non-Equity Jeff Awards, including New Adaptation and Best Production; his adaptation of Neil Gaiman's NEVERWHERE received the Non-Equity Jeff Award for New Adaptation; and his version of Oscar Wilde's THE PICTURE OF DORIAN GRAY was nominated for New Adaptation. He was commissioned by the Illinois Shakespeare Festival in 2010 to produce a new adaptation of Dumas' THE THREE MUSKETEERS, and two of his plays have been published by Playscripts, Inc.

WWW.ROBERTKAUZLARIC.COM

ABOUT LIFELINE THEATRE

Lifeline Theatre is driven by a passion for story. The ensemble process supports writers in the development of literary adaptations and new work, while their theatrical and educational programs foster a lifelong engagement with literature and the arts. A cultural anchor of the Rogers Park neighborhood in Chicago, they are committed to deepening their connection to an ever-growing family of artists and audiences, both near and far.

Lifeline Theatre's history of extraordinary world premiere adaptations includes MainStage productions of NORTHANGER ABBEY, PRIDE & PREJUDICE, THE OVERCOAT, THE LEFT HAND OF DARKNESS, THE TALISMAN RING, JANE EYRE, CAT'S CRADLE, AROUND THE WORLD IN 80 DAYS, THE KILLER ANGELS, A ROOM WITH A VIEW, THE ISLAND OF DR. MOREAU, THE MARK OF ZORRO, MARIETTE IN ECSTASY, NEVERWHERE, THE MOONSTONE, WATERSHIP DOWN, and THE COUNT OF MONTE CRISTO.

Lifeline also produced world premiere adaptations of J. R. R. Tolkein's THE LORD OF THE RINGS TRILOGY (THE FELLOWSHIP OF THE RING, THE TWO TOWERS, AND THE RETURN OF THE RING) and four installments of the Dorothy L. Sayers Lord Peter Wimsey mysteries (WHOSE BODY?, STRONG POISON, GAUDY NIGHT, and BUSMAN'S HONEYMOON).

Family MainStage productions have included A WRINKLE IN TIME, LIZARD MUSIC, THE SNARKOUT BOYS AND THE AVACADO OF DEATH, THE PHANTOM TOLLBOOTH, JOURNEY OF THE SPARROWS, THE SILVER CHAIR, JOHNNY TREMAIN, and TREASURE ISLAND.

In 1986 Lifeline inaugurated its KidSeries program. Productions have included MR. POPPER'S PENGUINS, MIKE MULLIGAN AND HIS STEAM SHOVEL, BUNNICULA, JAMES AND THE GIANT PEACH, THE STORY OF FERDINAND, MRS. PIGGLE-WIGGLE, MY FATHER'S DRAGON, CLICK CLACK MOO: COWS THAT TYPE, THE STINKY CHEESE MAN, DUCK FOR PRESIDENT, THE TRUE STORY OF THE 3 LITTLE PIGS!, THE VELVETEEN RABBIT, THE LAST OF THE DRAGONS, and ARNIE THE DOUGHNUT.

Plays commissioned by Lifeline Theatre have gone on to publication, numerous regional and national tours, and to more than a hundred subsequent productions across over forty U.S. states, five Canadian provinces, as well as in England and Ireland.

FOR MORE INFORMATION
VISIT WWW.LIFELINETHEATRE.COM

lifeline
THEATRE
Big Stories, Up Close

OTHER PLAYS FROM SORDELET INK

THE MOONSTONE
by Robert Kauzlaric
adapted from the novel by Wilkie Collins

THE COUNT OF MONTE CRISTO
by Christoper M Walsh
adapted from the novel by Alexandre Dumas

A TALE OF TWO CITIES
by Christoper M Walsh
adapted from the novel by Charles Dickens

SEASON ON THE LINE
by Shawn Pfautsch
adapted from Herman Melville's MOBY-DICK

ONCE A PONZI TIME
by Joe Foust

IT CAME FROM MARS
by Joseph Zettelmaier

EBENEEZER - A CHRISTMAS PLAY
by Joseph Zettelmaier

THE GRAVEDIGGER: A FRANKENSTEIN PLAY
by Joseph Zettelmaier
adapted from the novel by Mary Shelly

THE SCULLERY MAID
by Joseph Zettelmaier

DEAD MAN'S SHOES
by Joseph Zettelmaier

ALL CHILDISH THINGS
by Joseph Zettelmaier

EVE OF IDES
by David Blixt

Made in the USA
Middletown, DE
23 August 2017